FROM THE
BUREAU
TO THE
BOARDROOM

FROM THE
BUREAU
TO THE
BOARDROOM

30 MANAGEMENT LESSONS FROM THE FBI

DAN CARRISON

AMACOM

American Management Association

New York • Atlanta • Brussels • Chicago • Mexico City • San Francisco
Shanghai • Tokyo • Toronto • Washington, D.C.

Special discounts on bulk quantities of AMACOM books are available to corporations, professional associations, and other organizations. For details, contact Special Sales Department, AMACOM, a division of American Management Association, 1601 Broadway, New York, NY 10019.
Tel: 212-903-8316. Fax: 212-903-8083.
E-mail: specialsls@amanet.org
Website: www.amacombooks.org/go/specialsales
To view all AMACOM titles go to: www.amacombooks.org

This publication is designed to provide accurate and authoritative information in regard to the subject matter covered. It is sold with the understanding that the publisher is not engaged in rendering legal, accounting, or other professional service. If legal advice or other expert assistance is required, the services of a competent professional person should be sought.

Library of Congress Cataloging-in-Publication Data

Carrison, Dan.
    From the bureau to the boardroom : 30 management lessons from the FBI / Dan Carrison.
        p. cm.
    Includes index.
    ISBN-13: 978-0-8144-1063-9 (hardcover)
    ISBN-10: 0-8144-1063-4 (hardcover)
        1. United States. Federal Bureau of Investigation—Management.
    2. Management—Case studies.   3. Leadership—Case studies.   I. Title.
    HV8144.F43C37 2009
    658—dc22

                                                        2008033520

Printing number

10   9   8   7   6   5   4   3   2   1

Dedicated to Executive Editor Adrienne Hickey, who shepherded me through my first three books with AMACOM.

Happy retirement, Adrienne.

Contents

Introduction

The responsibilities of the Federal Bureau of Investigation (FBI) are so profound, in terms of the national consequences of failure, that it seems to have little in common with the less dramatically challenged companies and corporations the rest of us serve—other than the obvious structural similarities (chain of command, a central headquarters, multiple branches, payroll department, receptionist at the front lobby, etc.).

But the FBI, for all its gravitas, deals with management issues no different from our own. It competes on a global playing field, facing cross-cultural challenges that would seem very familiar to us. It must operate with limited resources and win with the tools it has, not with the tools it wishes it had. It must manage failure and its resulting effect on morale. It must try to retain its top performers, who are receiving unmatchable offers from outside the organization. It must perpetuate an organizational culture within an increasingly diverse workforce. And it is under constant pressure to perform.

Having worked with the FBI once before, on a chapter for a previous book, I was granted access to agents, supervisors, and executives throughout the chain of command and was able to hear exciting stories of management crises and resolutions. It's a wonder that no one has ever written a business management book that posited the FBI as an organizational model. It's about time somebody did.

The FBI is a terrific organizational model—not because of

1

the nature of its work, but because of the ways its work is managed. This is one of the reasons retiring agents can move so seamlessly into the private sector and why active agents receive lucrative offers from high-performance companies. The management techniques that took down the Mob and the KGB—and that are now working so effectively in the war against terror—work equally well when applied to leading a company. They would work, in fact, if only half applied.

Over the decades, in its daily struggle against crime and terror, the Federal Bureau of Investigation has developed a number of powerful leadership and management principles. Happily, these principles and techniques can be applied quite effectively to our own daily struggle in the competitive marketplace—without even firing a shot.

1

Managing the Corporate Mission

Encourage the acceptance of new roles • Implement an up-or-out management policy • Make management an attractive option to your top performers • Ensure that the day-to-day lives up to the mission

> After 9/11 it was clear that we needed to fundamentally change the way we do business.
>
> —FBI DIRECTOR ROBERT S. MUELLER

Imagine being Robert Mueller on September 11, 2001. He had been the newly appointed Director of the FBI for all of one week. Suddenly America was under attack, on his watch. Three planes had hit their targets, another had reportedly crashed, and hundreds of planes were still in the air, any one of which could have been under the control of suicidal hijackers. Outside his office window in the nation's capital, he could see the Pentagon, the very symbol of American military might, in flames. On the television screen, the landmark twin towers of the World Trade Center had defied imagination by collapsing upon an untold number of first responders and the people they had been trying so valiantly to save.

While the FBI had been taking down the Mafia; thwarting the attempts of international cocaine cartels to establish beachheads on American soil; stemming the alarming proliferation of a whole new breed of vicious, sociopathic street gangs; and chasing down bank robbers, kidnappers, software piracy rings, and identity theft gangs, a deadly adversary in the shadows of Arabia had been planning an unthinkable outrage.

Imagine the weight of his responsibilities as the smoke cleared. His job would have been difficult enough, overseeing the Bureau's fifty-six branch offices, sixty global offices, ten thousand agents, and eighteen thousand support personnel. But now the President of the United States had mandated revolutionary change. Director Mueller not only had to run the FBI, but he had to immediately reorganize it to meet the greatest threat to the general population in American history.

Few executives have ever been so challenged.

Robert Mueller's agency had been given a new directive by the President of the United States. The FBI's traditional role as a domestic law enforcement agency had been redefined and expanded; national security would now become its top priority. Sweeping changes were about to be implemented, virtually overnight, in a tradition-rich, global organization with "bureaucracy" for its middle name—the Federal *Bureau* of Investigation.

Encourage the Acceptance of New Roles

The new paradigm laid down by Director Mueller after 9/11 amounted to a major reorganization of the Bureau and a new forward strategy. Assistant Director Stephen Tidwell remembers that day very well.

"Director Mueller flopped my world," he says with understated simplicity.

"Our responsibilities used to be essentially domestic; now they were global. We used to be all about law enforcement; now we're about national security *and* law enforcement. We used to be case-driven; now we're threat-driven. Our inclination used to be 'Restrict, and share what we must'; and now it's 'Share, and restrict what we must.' Budget used to drive the strategy; now strategy drives the budget. Our priorities had changed as well. Number one was now counterterrorism. Number two: counterintelligence. Number three: cyber. You didn't get to 'crime,' per se, until number four—and even that had changed into a focus on public corruption."

Sitting across the polished mahogany boardroom table, attired in a suit, with a pleasant smile on his face, Tidwell looked every bit the consummate senior executive. I interviewed him on his last day as head of the Los Angeles field office. He was flying back to Washington, D.C., to assume the duties of executive assistant director of the FBI's criminal, cyber, response, and services branch. In 2005, he was the recipient of the Presidential Rank Award for Meritorious Executive. When he mentioned to me that his assigned street role during his early days with the Bureau had been that of a "hit man and thug," I naturally tried to imagine this award-winning executive in the role of a hit man during a sting operation, or as a thug—coldly menacing in a three-piece suit, or unshaven and brutish in a leather jacket. And yes, suddenly I could see it! It was in his eyes, mainly, but just for a fleeting instant.

"The organizational changes," he continued, "were major. But we adjusted quickly."

Stephen Tidwell, in his twenty-fourth year with the Bureau, has seen major shifts in strategy before. "At various points in our history we've been given a new mission, and we've adapted. I can give you two examples that I've experienced personally. I joined the FBI in 1983, when the Bureau was given concurrent jurisdiction with the Drug Enforcement Agency. That was a big change for the FBI. We suddenly went from wearing suits to getting down and dirty and doing jump-outs in the street, arresting crack cocaine dealers. Then the FBI's role was expanded again in the early 90s, when we were told to take out the gangs. That was another big change, infiltrating the street gangs.

"We did it with drugs, we did it with gangs, and now we're being asked to do it with terrorism."

In field offices all across the nation, special agents in charge—the FBI's equivalent of a branch executive—assembled the troops and explained Director Mueller's new paradigm. Going after the terrorists, of course, was not a hard sell to dedicated agents who had taken the attacks on the homeland personally. But even so, there must have been those for whom the announcement was unsettling. After all, taking down a criminal enterprise so that not one brick is left standing can take years, and thousands of agents were heavily invested in their life's work. It had taken them a chunk of their career just to develop their network of informants and contacts. It had taken years just to identify who was who in the secretive criminal families they had patiently infiltrated, at the risk of their lives. What was to become of all of their hard work? Would their casebooks be turned over to a stranger who would waltz in from another agency? Would that stranger be as good as they were? Would the drug dealer, or the pedophile, or the vicious leader of a gang walk free because the last few steps of a long-term investigation were mishandled by a newcomer?

These questions were handled with sensitivity by FBI managers, who were, after all, on the street themselves not so many years ago. Many agents were allowed to see their "pet" investigations through to conclusion and even to remain in their particular area of investigations; others were asked to hand off their cases and transition to the antiterror squads. One thing was made clear to all: The priorities may have changed, but not the need for FBI core expertise. "It's not as if the traditional FBI training was suddenly rendered irrelevant by the new priorities," explains Tidwell. "We could, in fact, fall back on that training and on that core expertise, because terrorist cells have much in common with criminal enterprises. They have trainers, finance people, transportation people, facilitators, suppliers, bomb makers, recruiters, etc. We just had to recalibrate, not reinvent the wheel. But this is an extraordinarily resilient organization. It doesn't take long before the adjustment becomes 'core.' And of course part of that is generational: we have people in the Bureau today that weren't here before 9/11."

How well have the FBI agents adapted to their new role? "When the public asks us, 'What have you been doing in the war against terror?'" concludes Tidwell, "we can't really answer that in specifics. What we *can* tell the public is this: 'We haven't been hit again in six years.' "

I left the interview thinking that of all the unintended consequences of the terrorist attack on 9/11—the patriotic response, the national solidarity, the overthrow of the Taliban in Afghanistan, the war in Iraq—the one the terrorists may most regret will be the shift in the priorities of the Federal Bureau of Investigation.

Accepting New Roles in Private Enterprise

When change threatens, we are all conservatives. It is human nature to assume that an oncoming transformation of the corporate culture will be a change for the worse, especially if there is little communication from on high. But even change for the better can disrupt the rhythm of our lives. And certainly when change is portended and mysterious and as yet indefinable, employees become anxious. An IT guru who hears of an impending merger with another company, which will impose its own superior proprietary information system, balks at the thought. Today his associates come to him with questions; he enjoys the prestige of being a guru. Tomorrow he will be as uninformed as everyone else. He will be back at square one, having to learn a whole new process.

The salesperson who has heard credible whispers of an imminent change in product line or sales territory or market segment loses sleep at night because she, too, is heavily invested in the present. What will happen to all the relationships she has cultivated over the years? She can hear her competition crowing in triumph! An expert on her current product, she will have to go back to basic training for the new line. She will have to start all over again, like an entry-level employee right out of college, except that she has the income needs of a family breadwinner. And with a change in job description comes a change in performance metrics—as if they weren't already difficult enough!

How senior leadership announces and manages upcoming change is very important to how it will be received. Communication from a trusted voice within the organization is all important, because if employees are not officially informed, they will inform themselves. Rumors will spread of their own accord; if they are unanswered by management, the credibility of the whispers will only increase: "It must be true; otherwise management would deny it." If it weren't so serious, the damage a rumor can cause would be laughable considering that the actions taken in response are so often based on falsehoods. Résumés have been faxed on the heels of totally unfounded gossip. As word has gotten out into the marketplace, company stock has been unloaded simply because of hearsay. And customers—on the assumption that "where there's smoke, there's fire"—have discovered alternate sources of supply, all because senior management has either remained mum or has not been forthcoming about the upcoming dynamic and about the employees' new place within it.

But employees' reaction to impending change need not be based on fear. It's very possible that a company employee may have a proprietary view of his or her work, precisely because he or she is very good at it. The ease of transfer will depend upon the degree to which employees consider their work important. We see "hands-on" managers all the time in the workplace who, despite being promoted, will not relinquish responsibility; they continue to do the work their subordinate has been hired to do. Their inability to let go is not selfish—indeed, their obsessive nature only increases their workload—but because they think nobody else can do the job as well. Change for dedicated people like these is tantamount to divorce.

And even if an employee is not particularly expert in his job, he may feel that he is best suited for his current task, not for the one in the offing. A new job description, then, is to him the harbinger of failure. He knows himself. He has found his niche, and now it is being taken away.

In all these cases, and in countless others that are easily imagined, not knowing how one will "fit" in the new paradigm is the worst part. The other shoe hasn't yet fallen, and until it does, every workday will be a time of anxiety. If management lets this happen, it has only itself to blame.

Senior leadership must make it clear that the upcoming change is across the board, affecting everybody—not just *you*. The change must be presented as evolutionary, not arbitrary, and important to the organization's ability to excel in the future. Because it will require new skills, the change will increase the professional capacity of every employee, thereby increasing employees' value to the organization. In that sense the new paradigm will be résumé enhancing, increasing the employee's value to the entire industry.

This suggestion that change can promote personal growth is intimidating to those who do not wish to grow. Comfort zones are generally productive; the employee has already spent the time needed to get up to speed and is now on track and does not wish to deviate. Management might want to encourage such an employee to step back a moment and look at this new company development in a biographical perspective. All the previous changes along his or her career path were also traumatic, but they led to a greater skill set, job security, and more income for the family. Self-actualization is a worthy goal in itself, but it also generally pays off. This new dynamic, then, should be embraced. Like the others, it will be a change for the better.

Just as Stephen Tidwell reminded his agents that their core expertise would serve them well in meeting the new challenges, so too must management make it clear that customer service is customer service whatever the product, that sales skills are universal, and that the critical thinking learned on the current job will continue to lead toward solutions under the new regime. While it may not be literally true that "there is nothing new under the sun," it is practically true.

One of the best ways to put the butterflies of the rank and file into formation is to assign learning tasks as soon as possible so that the employees become immersed in the new subject matter. It might also be wise of management to introduce its key players to new role models who deal well with the new challenges about to be imposed and who had to go through the learning process themselves. When well represented by management, the announcement of impending change should gladden the hearts of all concerned because it will signify liberation of the employee's talents and new life for the organization.

Communication from the top is everything. Most CEOs do not have fifty-six branch offices; they should take note that Director Mueller has visited *all* of the Bureau's field offices, and some several times. "Each time," says Joe Ford, COO of the FBI (the position itself an innovation of Mueller's), "he talks with the folks there and reveals his vision of the Bureau. Everyone sees him and can talk to him. He's also in the habit of webcasting town hall meetings, where he can field questions from the rank and file."

If Director Mueller can visit every branch and at the same time manage his daily briefings with the President of the United States and oversee the FBI's efforts in several global theaters of war (against drugs, gangs, the Mob, terrorists, etc.), even the hardest-working CEO can surely find the time to communicate the implications of impending change to his or her rank and file and put their anxiety to rest.

Implement an Up-or-Out Management Policy

On October 21, 2007, *The Philadelphia Inquirer* ran an article written by staff reporter John Shiffman that expressed the community's dismay over the imminent departure of two veteran FBI violent crime and public corruption supervisors from the Philadelphia field office. The experienced agents had, it seems, chosen retirement rather than comply with an internal policy that would have required them to relocate to FBI headquarters in Washington, D.C., or return to the beat as street agents and suffer a pay cut. Shiffman expressed his own concern, and that of a number of commissioners and community leaders, about the unintended consequences of a management policy that seemed to jeopardize the effectiveness, at least in the short term, of the local FBI office. Similar articles appear occasionally in cities all over the nation. According to Shiffman, no less than 576 squad supervisors nationwide have been given the identical choice to date. "About half have refused to move to Washington. Of those, 150 have returned to the streets and 135 have retired. An additional 260 supervisors will face the same choice next year."

One of the defining characteristics of Director Mueller's leadership style is his resurrection of the FBI's "up-or-out" policy, which had not always been enforced under previous administrations. Under this policy, an FBI supervisor (middle manager) may not sit at his or her desk for more than five years. He or she must either "move up" into higher management or "move out" of that supervisory role and go back on the street as a field agent.

The program is not without controversy. Moving "up" generally means relocation for a tour of duty at FBI headquarters followed by an assignment in another part of the nation. Not all supervisors are keen on the prospect of moving. There are any number of reasons for wanting to stay at a particular desk. Perhaps the supervisor is doing a bang-up job dismantling criminal enterprises and wishes to continue doing so; perhaps investigations that have taken years are just now beginning to bear fruit; maybe it has taken the supervisor five years to really get familiar with the domain; or perhaps the supervisor's teams are really just now starting to click. Often the objections to relocating are based on financial concerns. It is likely the FBI agent is not the "breadwinner" of the family. Most, in fact, have taken a significant pay cut to become an agent. In many marriages, the agent's spouse contributes most of the family income, and relocation could certainly mean the loss of that income and the interruption of a career. Other factors must be considered, such as taking the children out of schools they love and away from friends at an age when friendships are vitally important to them. Joe Ford, the FBI's COO, estimates "roughly 50 percent of the supervisors have stepped up and gone into higher level management positions. The other 50 percent have either returned to being a street agent or retired."

Although this "either-or" transition mandate seems hard on the field supervisor, the Bureau is implementing a far-reaching management policy that has had a notable history of success.

The U.S. military services have implemented an up-or-out management policy within their officer corps for two hundred years. Any former "military brat" can recall being uprooted time and again as his or her father or mother kept pace with periodic reassignments—and with their corresponding increases in responsibility and professional capacity—every two to three years. The nomadic life is rough on the children, who are the perennial "new kids on the block" in far-flung communities, and it is difficult for the spouses, who must leave their jobs and bid farewell to friends almost as soon as the relationships are established.

But it is good for the organization.

With their unrelenting pressure to perform, the U.S. Army, Navy, Air Force, and Marine Corps have nourished and cultivated an officer corps that is the envy of the world and, perhaps more importantly, is a senior leadership team of warriors, not bureaucrats. A deaf ear would be turned to the devoted followers of a particular officer who begged for their charismatic captain to remain with the ship or their beloved colonel to continue his command of the battalion. Such charismatic leaders must move up in the organization for the good of all. And they are replaceable. The military has demonstrated over two centuries that equally talented leaders wait in the wings for their opportunity to inspire similarly devoted followers. And it's no different inside the FBI.

If an up-or-out management policy works well for the military and for the FBI—organizations that have a manager corps generally committed for a career—it is all the more important for a company in free enterprise, with its much more fluid management base. That magnetic manager in the Chicago office is a free agent who receives lucrative offers from the competition regularly; he or she could leave the company any day. The talent waiting in the wings, which is also susceptible to being stolen away by the competition, must be given its chance. One never knows when the "backup quarterback" will be needed.

But promoting an up-or-out policy requires sensitivity. Even mature adults can be unaware of their own fear of change and refuse to recognize that the pressure to move up a notch in management can be very constructive in terms of personal growth. How many of us have accepted a promotion with great trepidation—certain we were not ready for it—only to find a whole new world before us and an unprecedented appreciation of the big picture? In how many biographies have we read about coaches pushing their athletic protégés to achieve their God-given potential or of teachers urging their reluctant students to glory? How many children have been led kicking and screaming into experiences they will treasure forever? How many of us, as adults, are now eternally grateful to those who have pulled us up to their level?

An up-or-out management program prods the successful toward continued success but at higher levels of influence, where they belong. It also undermines the ability of the rank and file to complain of inexperienced managers at the corporate level, because the kinds of people who should be in higher management—the experienced and proven supervisors—have been asked.

Pick an organization at random and one of the most common complaints voiced by middle management will likely be that "headquarters is out of touch." If that is so, the remedy would surely be to take some of those streetwise middle managers to headquarters so the organization at the highest level can benefit from their considerable experience. But if the middle managers refuse to go, how can they continue to complain that headquarters is out of touch? They are themselves the cure.

It would be a disservice to the organization to allow any

manager, no matter how effective or inspiring, to occupy her desk for as long as she is doing an excellent job. How will the younger talent be cultivated if a supervisor clings to her role indefinitely? An up-or-out policy is a proven success. Once set in stone, it will push that ensconced manager into higher levels of responsibility and service or back into her previous role. Either way, her desk will be vacated for the new generation's leader, and the organization will benefit.

Make Management an Attractive Option to Your Top Performers

In private enterprise, an upward move into management is almost always associated with a raise. When the employee comes home and proudly proclaims, "Honey, I got that promotion!" the spouse also rejoices because it means more money. But imagine if the "promotion" was not accompanied by a raise in salary. One's sanity would be questioned for accepting more responsibility, more stress, and longer hours for nothing. Yet this is pretty much the case in the FBI—except that in addition to the increased workload, the promotion often requires the whole family to pull up stakes and relocate.

Tim McNally, in his long career in the Bureau, went up the organizational ladder from street agent, to supervisor, to assistant agent in charge, to an inspector's position at headquarters, to special agent in charge (SAC) for the Baltimore field office, and finally to SAC for the Los Angeles office—while many of his associates chose to remain street agents for their entire (and exciting) careers. "Unlike the private sector," explains Tim, "historically the Bureau did not offer the economic incentives to move up the line and accept multiple transfers. In prior generations, you moved up the line for a variety of motives. Many were recognized in the field as having great potential and were pushed to move forward. Some were ambitious and wanted to pursue higher-level positions. Some were hell-bent on improving the organization and had the ability to lead and were selfless in their dedication to the organization."

But many agents prefer to stay where they are, finding the necessity to relocate not only tremendously inconvenient for the entire family, but damaging economically when the spouse is a professional in his or her own right and earning an income that would be difficult to replace. In addition to the inconvenience, there are many agents who just love "working the street." This is why they joined the FBI: to catch bank robbers, tear down criminal enterprises, disrupt drug cartels, and break up street gangs that have terrorized entire neighborhoods. That senior leaders are able to get as many street agents as they do to accept the responsibilities and the inconveniences of management without significant pay increases is a real testimonial to their powers of persuasion, as well as to the strength of the commitment of the individual agents.

Just as there are many FBI agents who prefer to work the street rather than take a job as a manager, there are top performers in every company who abhor the idea of going into management and who dread being asked. From the organization's point of view, however, the top performer may be precisely the person who should supervise and inspire others to perform as well as he or she has. The resulting tension is generally the fault of the organization. Had senior management handled its star employee properly, he or she would have jumped at the chance.

Why would top performers not want to go into management? The answer is simple: Their experiences of being managed have not been particularly inspiring. In fact, it is very possible that a company's best front-line employees have a low opinion of their managers, if not outright contempt. Why would they want to become managers?

It is the irony of ironies that so many companies cannot understand why one of their own would not want to join the management team when it is that very management team that has dissuaded the top performer from ever becoming a manager.

Let's examine some of the possible associations a high-performance employee may harbor toward management: (a) they are the "suits" who are nowhere to be found during the trials and tribulations of a project but who suddenly appear at its successful conclusion to take the credit; (b) they push from behind a desk instead of "pulling" their subordinates in the wake of their leadership; (c) sequestered in their offices, they are out of touch with the customer, with the marketplace, and with their own subordinates; (d) they are a hindrance, not a help; (e) they are the "office weenies" who couldn't make a living on the front lines of the economy if they had to; (f) they do not produce but instead live off the production of others; (g) they are empire builders; (h) they are ass kissers.

Furthermore, the duties of a manager are seen as antithetical to personal achievement. The happy warriors on the front lines see their own managers as paper shufflers who spend most of their time filling out reports to send upline. They see a position in management as stressful, without the "fight or flight" opportunities available in the field. Managers, to them, sit on the "hot seat" and must answer to the even more industrious empire builders at the executive levels above. Many top performers would not volunteer for what they consider to be a useless and ultimately humiliating post. And in the case of a hotshot salesperson, a move into management may very well mean a drop in income.

The senior leadership of an organization must realize there is another competing and equally exclusive club in the organization—the "antimanagement" cadre of doers, who are frankly admired by the rank and file for their charisma and ability and who take pride in *not* being part of the administrative chain of command. They are the achievers, the life blood of the organization, self-consciously rebellious and proud of their accomplishments—most of which, they feel, were achieved in spite of management. To the rank and file, these go-getters are the modern embodiments of Robin Hood, taking the stolen credit from the aristocracy of the organization and returning it to the rightful owners: the workers. These respected top performers are privately, and sometimes openly, contemptuous of management.

But what if it were different? What if these frontline achievers so respected management that they couldn't wait to join its ranks—not for personal aggrandizement but for the opportunity to help lead the organization to greater heights?

If management were associated with action, and if being a manager meant the opportunity to slay even bigger dragons, the top performer couldn't wait for the promotion. If "management" meant being able to help one's associates, still fighting on the front line, to get their jobs done more efficiently, and if it meant the chance to build a stronger company, then top performers would see it as their duty to accept the position. And if they felt that a post in management would be part of a self-actualizing process that would increase their own professional capacity, the transition into management would seem natural, right, and inevitable.

The best way to attract the organization's best into management is to fill the ranks of management with the organization's best. The siphon of talent into management would be self-perpetuating because like attracts like. If a top performer idolized his or her boss—and if that boss had an equally high opinion of his or her own supervisor—leaders would circulate from the feet, through the heart, to the brain of the organization in no time. Just like in the FBI.

But so often there is a corps of managers and a corps of performers, and never the twain shall meet. It's almost as if the company has two leadership structures, one formal, the other informal. And in some organizations, this dichotomy can deteriorate into a kind of schizophrenia. Senior leadership can avoid this "illness" by welcoming into the ranks of management only those who have walked the walk—proven, frontline achievers with years of experience who already command the respect of their associates. Sadly, this philosophy is less apt to be implemented in the era of the Sarbanes-Oxley Act (SOX), when more and more leaders are selected for their knowledge of regulatory compliance issues, corporate law, and accounting procedures rather than for their company's core expertise. When bean counters, attorneys, and ethics officers lead the rank and file, the top performers will form their own group, a subculture of mutually respected achievers. While tolerating management, they will never enter its ranks. Worse for the organization, they will not pass the benefit of their considerable experience upline. The organization will continue to be led by those who have not, and cannot, walk the walk.

Ensure That the Day-to-Day Lives Up to the Mission

There are numerous ways to make sure that your day-to-day operations live up to your corporate mission. Two ways the FBI does this are to require their agents to periodically demonstrate their expertise and to have an extremely rigorous inspection program.

Require Your People to Periodically Demonstrate Their Core Expertise

Despite the increasing technical sophistication required of FBI agents in their battle against global terrorist organizations—especially in the areas of detection, surveillance, and the cyber-threat environment—the Director maintains the Bureau's tradition of requiring all agents to demonstrate their core expertise.

Whenever we see FBI agents in televised news conferences, we are apt to forget for a moment that they are, in fact, law enforcement officers. Dapper in business suits, articulate in speech, at ease in front of the camera, they seem more like government executives when standing next to the uniformed police, sheriff, or state trooper personnel gathered around the microphone. Unlike their paramilitary brethren, the FBI agents don't even appear to be armed. But holstered behind the well-pressed coats are deadly semiautomatics that have fired thousands of high-pressure .40-caliber rounds. FBI agents, all beneficiaries of perhaps the most intensive firearms training on the planet, are notorious for being crack shots. And the underworld knows this; even the most fearless gangbanger will immediately raise both hands at the words, "Halt. FBI!"

Despite the exhaustive firearms training at the Academy, all FBI agents, regardless of seniority, rank, or job description, must qualify with their weapons four times a year, every single year of their career. It matters not at all if an agent shot a perfect score on the previous qualification test or if he or she has a reputation in the field office as a "dead-eye"; he or she must prove it once again every three months. There are no exceptions to the rule. And one can expect no help from the range masters, who would not give their own flesh and blood the benefit of the doubt when tallying the score.

The purpose of the firearm requalification mandate is obvious. Whenever agents must use deadly force in defense of their own lives or the lives of others, it will be under emergency conditions, when muscle memory and complete familiarity with the firearm will serve them well. And, of course, the old adage "use it or lose it" applies. "These are perishable skills, which must be constantly nurtured," explains Academy firearms instructor Jeff Green. "The firearms training here at the Academy is the best in the world. I know of no other training program anywhere which requires the individual to shoot as many rounds downfield as we do [four thousand bullets!]. But even the best training can carry you for only so long; the skills must be continually reinforced."

There are more subtle benefits of the firearms requalification program that will be of interest to the business manager, who does not have to shoot it out with bank robbers and terrorists in the normal course of the day, and these have to do with the impact on the organizational culture of being required to periodically demonstrate core expertise.

For one thing, shooting the firearm under the pressure of a mandated exam surely must return every FBI agent to his or her "Academy days," no matter his or her seniority. There is something earnest, even humbling, in having to continually requalify with a skill that was taught in "basic" training. Firing the weapon for score is not something one can do in the privacy of the office, like taking an online exam. It must be done on a range, under the gaze of the range master and whoever else stands behind the line (like curious managers), as well as in front of one's fellow agents who are either practicing or requalifying. As the silhouette target is reeled in, everyone can see the score. To fail means one has to requalify twice the next time; failure again means having your gun taken away from you, not particularly career enhancing in a law enforcement agency, not to mention humiliating.

The requirement for requalification keeps FBI agents in touch with their raison d'etre, which is: "Every agent is an investigator." It must be remembered that there are FBI agents who, because of their job descriptions, are on a computer all day fighting cyber crime, or going through the accounting ledgers of a business under investigation, or researching money laundering, or investigating public corruption, or sitting behind a desk as a manager. These agents are not, in their normal business day, kicking down doors and arresting fugitives. Yet if fellow agents on a violent crime squad need help on a particular operation, these "white collar" agents will immediately drop what they're doing and lend a hand. The rough-and-ready squad supervisor does not for a moment consider these office-bound agents to be a liability as he deploys them into harm's way. He knows that within the past three months they have proven yet again that they can shoot the black out of the bull's-eye.

It must be a great comfort to know, as an FBI manager, that any agent you happen to tap on the shoulder for an assignment shares the fundamental core expertise of his or her calling. It must also be a great comfort for every rank-and-file agent to know that any associate, chosen at random, can back him or her up in a life-or-death situation. How do these agents know this? Because all have had to prove it to the Bureau, and by implication to all of their comrades, through the quarterly requalification firearms testing program.

The question is: Do you have a similar level of confidence in the core expertise of the people in your company, or—to narrow it down to a reasonable expectation—in your own department?

It's a safe bet that many senior executives would be surprised, if not shocked, at the degree to which the fundamentals, in terms of product and service offerings unique to the company, are not shared even among team members, much less disparate employees throughout the organization. And there are some legitimate reasons for this. Some employees are brought in from other industries for the skills they offer—such as an accountant from the aerospace industry who now works for an automobile manufacturer—without going through basic employee training at the new company.

"Turnover" is also an issue. Many employees are new and have not yet been grounded in the corporate culture. The increasing demand for specialization can also keep employees so focused on their own particular bailiwick that their broad-based knowledge atrophies. Outsourcing is another impediment to employee product-service knowledge, because once a function is delegated to others, so too is the responsibility for keeping "up to speed."

One of the best ways to determine whether or not "requalification" of certain core company skills is necessary is to gauge the employee's reaction to the proposition. Chances are there would be a rebellion at the very suggestion. There are fifteen-year veterans in every company who have been trained once; they are not going to be receptive to being tested fifteen years later. There are salespeople who sell a product but cannot "demo" it. There are receptionists who know every telephone extension in the office but do not have the foggiest notion of what the company does. There are customer service techs who haven't the slightest idea of the features and benefits soon to be released. And there are executives who have so lost touch with the products and services of the company that they might as well be dwelling in a castle in the sky.

This is why an intelligent customer so often knows more about the products and services than the employees at the company offering those products and services and why the customer almost certainly knows more about the trends in the industry in general.

Senior leadership in private enterprise might want to consider implementing a core expertise testing program that would require employees to periodically prove themselves. The FBI does it, and there is no rebellion from the ranks. Even though the agents are already working ungodly hours on their investigations and might rather skip a requalification test (and the practice time required to prepare for it), they would acknowledge that the Bureau is entitled to know if all of its agents can handle a gun. Isn't the CEO of a company similarly entitled to have a fairly high level of confidence in the fundamental knowledge level of his or her employees?

Without some kind of testing program—or, when appropriate, a less formal feedback mechanism such as periodic lunches in which the conversation can delve deep into the subject matter—how will management know if its CPA is keeping current with pending SOX legislation, or if its software guru is up to speed with the latest threats from cyberspace, or if its salespeople can confidently demonstrate the newest versions of the product line? But job-specific core expertise is only part of the story. What about shared knowledge on the bedrock level? Firearm proficiency within the FBI, for example, is part of the DNA of the agency, a skill set every agent has in common with another. From that point on, each goes into his or her special area of investigation, learning skills that are not necessarily held in common. Were it not for the basic tactical knowledge all agents share, as investigators first, the FBI could easily expand into multiple realms beyond the pull of its own gravity.

A private and publicly held organization similarly requires the bond of commonly held knowledge if it is to retain its core identity and present a credible front to the marketplace and to the customer. At a bare minimum, every employee should be familiar with the company's legacy and with the names and backgrounds of the key executive leaders. The basic competitive advantages of the product line should also be common knowledge; any employee with a telephone at his or her desk should be able to, in broad terms, carry on an intelligent, if brief, conversation with any customer who happens to get the wrong extension. And a general knowledge of the marketplace, and of the company's place within it, is not too much to ask of every employee.

There are so many resources the employee can avail himself of, from intracompany bulletins, to industry publications, to informative blogs on the Internet. But without a little pressure from on high, many will not take the initiative. And unless they are firmly grounded in the company's offerings—and familiar with the products and services of its competitors and with the dynamic changes taking place in the industry—they will lose credibility in the eyes of the customer. They will forever be in the awkward position of having to tell a discerning client, "I'll get back to you with the answer."

From the customer's standpoint, there are few things more impressive and more confidence inspiring than encountering a company where just about everyone seems to belong, as if each employee grew up in the organization. This is especially important today, in the age of outsourcing, when trying to get a simple answer to a simple question can be so frustrating. Shared company knowledge is so unexpected that when customers discover it, they think they have stumbled upon one organization in a million. A basic familiarity of the corporate mission, and of the company's offerings, that is shared throughout the rank and file is a tremendous competitive advantage.

A Rigorous Inspection Program Is Win-Win

There is a perception on the part of the general public—or, one should say, on the part of the taxpayer—that government employment is a refuge from the real world. Anyone who has shuffled through long lines at the Department of Motor Vehicles only to finally confront a clerk who has come to hate the human race has probably marveled at the lack of accountability for discourteous, indifferent customer service. "If that clerk worked for me," we mutter, "he wouldn't be working for me." Not only are we personally affronted by the lack of customer service, it has violated our sense of fair play. We work at the pleasure of our employers and our customers. We can be fired any day, while it seems to take an act of Congress to terminate a federal, state, or city employee. We are exposed to the elements of the free market, but they are sheltered by an impenetrable, abiding bureaucracy.

It is natural for us, then, to assume that government employees, in general, are under little meaningful pressure from their own management to perform. If a person can't be fired (barring some truly egregious offense), he or she cannot be motivated, like the rest of us, by the implicit threat of termination. When management is "all bark and no bite," what purpose would a lot of administrative posturing serve?

But if the truth were known, many federal agencies—the FBI in particular—exercise quite a bit of executive oversight. In fact, the Bureau has instituted an in-house inspection program so stringent that it is considered adversarial by its own management team. In the words of more than one manager, the Bureau's inspection process has been characterized as evidence of the FBI's willingness "to eat its own."

Every couple of years, an FBI field office will be subjected to a visit from headquarters, in the person of an inspector and his staff, who are there to determine how efficiently that branch is being managed. Although the inspector is an FBI veteran, quite likely an old friend of the SAC of the branch being evaluated, the inspector now seems a stranger to his comrade in arms. His staff, though pleasant, is equally estranged; they go about their duties with the dispassionate air of angels taking inventory in the Garden of Eden after the Fall of Man.

The inspections are designed to examine each performance metric relevant to the branch management team's operational efficiency and effectiveness. The process is so detailed that an inspection of a major field office, like the one in New York City, can require an inspection staff of 140 auditors and take as long as a month! The end result of any inspection could be the unflattering reassignment of the branch executive and/or members of his or her management team. "I don't know of any governmental agency that is tougher on its own than the FBI," says retired agent Tim McNally. "The only parallel I can think of is the military."

Tim should know. He's been on both sides of the process; he's been "inspected" and he's done the "inspecting." "It's a rather aggressive and tough process," he explains, "and not always popular with the managers of the field offices. But it's probably the best way to provide the big picture to senior management back at headquarters. They read those inspection reports and have a good idea of what's going on at that particular field office, not only from an anecdotal standpoint, but statistically. You're looking at how a branch allocates its resources and how it is working the priorities set by the Director. Since counterterrorism is the number one priority, an inspector will look carefully at a branch to see if its resources are accordingly utilized on that priority. If not, the people there have to explain why those resources have been delegated elsewhere."

Obviously, an inspector has to have been around the block before he or she is in a position to evaluate veteran FBI executives and managers who are on the front lines. "I had sixteen years of experience as a street agent, field supervisor, and as an assistant agent in charge before I was asked to become an inspector. And that's pretty typical; most inspectors have fifteen to twenty years of experience under their belts."

Even with his considerable experience, Tim realized the benefits of being able to look at the organization from altitude. "I spent a good portion of my career working a variety of cases in public corruption, organized crime, and international drug trafficking around the country, but until I became an inspector I didn't have the big picture." He capped off his twenty-four-year career with the FBI as the SAC of the Los Angeles field office—and, sure enough, his branch was inspected just like the others.

Although the compliance regulations of SOX have given the executive leadership of publicly held companies ample excuse for random audits of their departments and branches, a systematic, broad-based evaluation program of the management team is probably much more difficult to find—because neither side wants it. The field managers are not comfortable with the idea of being "inspected" because there is a presumption of distrust. There is also the clear indication that those on the front lines resent being inspected by a white-gloved staffer from corporate who is far removed from the front lines of the marketplace. Senior management may also not be particularly fond of the idea because it puts them in a bad light, perpetuating the patriarchal stereotype of overbearing leadership. And even if the execs are comfortable with being cast in that light, they may not be amenable to the costs of staff, logistical support, downtime at each branch, and the lost opportunities at each branch during the inspection. Neither does corporate want to give the impression it has serious enough questions about a manager to warrant a full-scale assessment.

On the presumption that "if it ain't broke don't fix it," evaluation visits from corporate headquarters are more likely scheduled in response to "red flags" raised in the reporting data submitted by a particular branch. The first red flag may prompt a phone call, and if the trend continues, the executive leadership board may dispatch an old hand to call on the branch and have a talk with the manager. But the old hand would not arrive with a drum roll and a judicious inspection staff. The call would be as muted as possible so that everyone would be comfortable. The old hand from corporate would be there to help identify the problem and to offer some friendly advice.

It should be remembered that FBI inspections are not particularly comfortable. "Even though the inspector has a strong résumé within the Bureau and has walked the walk," recalls Tim McNally, "and even though he may personally know the management team at a particular field office, and everyone's shaking hands and smiling at his arrival, it is generally viewed as an adversarial relationship." Nor are FBI inspections reserved for field offices that have submitted reports indicative of a problem. There are fifty-six field offices in the nation, and all of them are periodically inspected, even a field office (as in McNally's case) under the command of a former FBI inspector!

There is a lot of merit to the concept of company-wide inspections focusing on management at the branch or departmental level, conducted by experienced veterans of the organization who are above cronyism. If the process is considered by the managers to be adversarial, they will take it seriously and prepare for it—and therein lies the main benefit of an inspection program: The department or branch will run like clockwork at the time of the inspection, and perhaps for months afterward, until entropy sets in.

The very fact that we feel compelled to prepare for an inspection underscores the need for one. We shouldn't have to prepare; the branch should already be running like clockwork under our leadership. Ideally, an inspector should be able to drop in at any time, unannounced, and find everything in order. And maybe, because of SOX compliance requirements, more departments are up to speed than ever before and can withstand an impromptu evaluation by a team of experts who know exactly what to look for and where to find it. In all likelihood, though, most managers would appreciate some time to prepare. And, having done that, they may very well survey the "finished product" and delight in what they see, a functioning, state-of-the-art enterprise that gobbles up and processes new business.

The nice thing about an upcoming, and heralded, inspection is that it puts the fear of God in all employees under the domain of the manager. *Everybody* must prepare for the inspection, and afterward, most will grudgingly admit they are better for it and more organized than ever before. An impending inspection also fosters a healthy "us vs. corporate" response from the branch about to be placed under the magnifying glass. Since the branch will pass or fail as a whole entity, simply getting one's individual area of responsibility will not be sufficient; one must help others get their areas organized. In doing so, an esprit de corps is developed. The "adversarial" relationship with corporate becomes good-natured as the team unites around a common cause and begins to display an attitude that clearly expresses to the inspector, "We defy you to find anything wrong with this branch."

There is nothing wrong with an inspector finding fault for comic effect where no fault exists. Marine Corps drill instructors, for example, are apt to conclude a flawless barracks inspection by grabbing a pillow off a perfectly made bed, throwing it on the spotless floor, and demanding to know, "What is *this* doing here?" The Marines standing at attention grin at the compliment; they know that the drill instructor (walking off in a feigned huff) couldn't find anything wrong.

A company-wide inspection program benefits the organization from the ground up. It allows senior leadership to see for itself whether or not the corporate vision has been properly communicated and is being properly implemented. How else would it really know? Certainly, the "numbers" submitted in the monthly branch reports are not sufficiently informative; numbers can be manipulated by the branch manager for some time before the truth will out. One way, admittedly, for management to see for itself would be the use of corporate spies, but a clandestine evaluation would not produce the universal preparation effect that is so beneficial to the branch. Corporate spies would also, when discovered, reinforce the presumption of distrust that senior management wishes to avoid.

When a forthright inspection program is unfeasible, some companies solicit feedback on managerial performance with the implementation of a 360-degree evaluation program. The anonymous feedback from an entire team or department is often frank and instructive. "Outlier" perspectives will be rounded out by the bell curve of the responses, and if the questionnaire is well designed, the portrait painted of the manager will be recognizable, if a bit abstract. The subjects of these periodic evaluations take them quite seriously; it is no coincidence that managers often bring doughnuts to the office on the day of the survey.

Even self-evaluations can be worthwhile, especially if the questions are sympathetically written in such a way that the manager is led down a path of introspection that is pleasingly enlightening. While few of us are going to be so scrupulously honest that management loses confidence in us, when continually pressed we will reveal (or hint at) our administrative weaknesses. A well-designed self-evaluation questionnaire is written almost in the manner of a lie detector test, with a number of variations of the same questions, coming from oblique angles. Sooner or later, we give up trying to outsmart the test and simply answer honestly, especially if we trust management to do the right thing. And this may be one area where a business will want to play softball where the FBI plays hardball. That is to say, the inspection process in private enterprise should not be intimidating. It should be clear to all concerned that management is there to help, not to make heads roll. When employees or managers fear the loss of their jobs, they will not be forthcoming.

When considering the FBI inspection program as a model for the business community, it must be remembered that the FBI inspector is not content to confine his evaluation to the inside of the field office. "We not only inspect inside the office," explains former inspector Rob Grant (now SAC of the Chicago office), "but outside. We talk to civic leaders, civil rights leaders, law enforcement officials, community leaders, and judges to learn their perception of the FBI." Similarly, the inspection in private enterprise should include conversations with key customers and major suppliers of the branch. Since good corporate citizenship should be part of the evaluation, the input of community leaders may also shed some light on the management style of the branch manager.

Finally, it should be emphasized that an inspection program creates a leadership pool of company inspectors who, though chosen for their considerable experience, have now rounded out their perspective of the organization and are ready to move on to the executive leadership team.

It really is a win-win concept. Steve Martinez, SAC of the Las Vegas field office, sums up the benefits of a rigorous inspection program this way: "I think it would be hard to find a SAC who didn't agree that they learned from the inspection process. Nobody likes it, particularly, but it makes us better executives, better leaders, and better managers."

CHAPTER TWO

Managing the Brand

Cultivating fidelity, bravery, and integrity in the workplace

It's so great to be in an organization where you have such a
high level of esteem for your associates.

—KRISTEN VON KLEINSMID, SUPERVISORY
SPECIAL AGENT, THREAT SQUAD

The motto of the FBI, immortalized on its dramatic seal, is "Fidelity, Bravery, Integrity." These are the kinds of noble words we would expect of an organization charged with the equally noble task of protecting the nation from terrorist attack and domestic crime. Would it seem presumptuous for a business enterprise to have such a grand motto? Surely most CEOs would shy away from the use of terms that would seem out of place when printed on the business cards of a company making widgets. But why? All three attributes—fidelity, bravery, and integrity—are needed in full measure to run any organization properly, including a business. Especially a business.

It would be difficult to rank the three attributes in terms of functional importance, although the FBI has done a good job of it. Certainly fidelity is something every organization wants of its employees, and vice versa. Bravery is a virtue that only momentarily seems inappropriate for most businesses, but it is precisely what is needed for one's employees to enable the company to prevail on the competitive battlefield of the marketplace. And of course integrity is critical to retaining public and internal trust. All three attributes can be cultivated, the FBI way.

Cultivating Fidelity in the Workplace

The FBI cultivates fidelity to the organization on an institutional level and on an interpersonal level.

Institutionally, the Bureau creates a strong desire to belong, while simultaneously instilling a credible doubt that membership is achievable. The prospective agents are put through an intense twenty-two-week training program that becomes a rite of passage. The candidates, for all their impressive civilian credentials, are not entirely confident they will make it through the Academy; many, in fact, will fail soon into the program. Until graduation, the "survivors" are uncredentialed agents in training who must walk around wearing plastic guns. The desire to become a member of the world's most respected law enforcement agency increases with each grueling day, giving new meaning to "sweat equity." All in it together, the prospective agents reach out to each other, helping wherever and whenever they can, and the bonds of friendship forged in this crucible can last a lifetime. When the graduation day finally comes, the presentation of the coveted FBI credential and badge is so meaningful that many choke up with emotion while taking the oath of allegiance.

Some of these goose bumps can be created, institutionally, in private enterprise.

While few companies can sustain or have practical need for a prolonged basic-training program, it is certainly possible to create a sense of gratitude and pride on the part of the employee for belonging to the organization. The key to accomplishing this is to make the entrance into the organization an achievement rather than a "done deal." This can be done through a serious interview process, an intense basic-training and/or orientation program, frequent team-building exercises, and a probationary period. FBI agents are on probation for two years, even after the best training in the world, and it is not a formality; there are some who do not make it through. Those agents who do eventually complete the two-year and twenty-two-week process are doubtless proud and relieved. After working so hard to become a member of the organization, an agent is not likely to treat his employment lightly.

Fidelity to the Bureau is also engendered on a much less formal, interpersonal level. Although the customs within the culture of the FBI are not thought of as managerial practices, the influence on the agent's view of the Bureau is undeniably powerful.

The FBI is a family. The degree of emotional and moral support freely and routinely exchanged by the agents and their support personnel in the Bureau will be difficult for many of us to relate to, including those of us who work for companies that proudly refer to themselves as "families." But this may be the key to the FBI's ability to engender faithfulness. During the interview process, I heard so many examples of the Bureau's support network in action that I became inured to the stories—until I realized how difficult it might be to match them, story for story, with examples from the normal workplace.

Marlo McGuire has been an FBI agent for only four years. She had a hint that the FBI might be a uniquely different organization to work for during the graduation ceremony at the Academy. At this grand, auspicious event—replete with the symbolism and tradition of a century of service—it seemed to her as if the Bureau never lost sight of what was important. Before the ceremony, the family members of the agents about to graduate were told, "If your child cries please don't feel you have to get up and leave. We know that your kids haven't seen mommy or daddy for twenty-two weeks, so of course they're going to cry. It's okay. Let 'em cry; we understand."

There is something revealing here about the FBI. Graduation ceremonies, generally speaking, are formal events, preceded by some kind of benediction and dignified speakers. Certainly graduation from the world's greatest law enforcement academy is a singular occasion, replete with flying flags, venerable symbols, and time-honored traditions. The Director himself may be present to deliver a commencement address. If the Bureau, in deference to the significance of the occasion, asked that family members leave their little children at home, it would not be deemed unreasonable. No one would expect or want the Director to compete with squalling babies.

The FBI, by allowing the entire family to attend the formal graduation ceremony and by asking the parents not to leave if the baby cries, is not resting on its laurels. Instead, it is enlisting the moral support of the most important people in the lives of the newly appointed agents. In some ways, this is also a graduation ceremony for the family members, who have endured twenty-two weeks of separation, and for the spouses who by themselves have had to run a household, raise the children, and face challenges usually handled by the absent husband or wife. By inviting the entire family to the very moving and emotional graduation ceremony (the babies are not the only ones who cry), the Bureau is acknowledging the existence and the importance of a whole corps of shadow managers who must sustain their spouses through the thick and thin of a demanding career. They have to be brought on board, too, and the Bureau knows it.

> Transferred to the Oakland field office, Marlo was not only new to the team, but to the city. "It's very unlikely you'll be assigned to your hometown," she explains, "so when you arrive at a field office in a strange city the people in that office become your family." Just how much so, she would soon learn.
>
> "While I was still relatively new with the Oakland office, my grandmother and aunt both passed away within two weeks of each other. So I asked my supervisor if I could take a few days off and attend the funerals. At each funeral, I was very moved to see six or seven of my coworkers, even though it meant travel for them. I didn't expect to see them, because I didn't want to burden anyone with my problems. But when I saw the faces of my fellow agents, I burst into tears. This is unlike any place I've ever worked. The emotional and moral support is incredible."
>
> Marlo's mother, Ethel, an FBI agent of twenty years, remembers the moment well. "I'm out of the Los Angeles office, so it was easier for me to attend. But even so, the cemetery was 125 miles away. Inside the funeral home, with my family members, I glanced up and saw in the back of the room my boss, several supervisors, and several agents from the LA office just standing there respectfully. I can't tell you how much that meant to me."

This kind of quiet demonstration of support, incidentally, is something that might not even occur to many of us in the workplace—not because we are indifferent to the grief of our associate, but because we would probably consider the death of a loved one to be a highly private matter. Indeed, we might even consider our presence at the funeral to be slightly invasive, as if we were overstepping the boundary between the personal and the professional. Certainly we would not be expected by our associate to attend. But consider the impact of seeing in the group of family members and close friends one's manager and coworkers—who have come on their own initiative and who keep a low and respectful profile, as if to say, "We are your close friends, too."

A year or so later, Marlo had a happier occasion to travel down to Los Angeles: She was getting married, to a man "outside" the Bureau. She had sent out a few notices, of course, as a courtesy, but "I never expected anybody to come, what with the travel, the hotels, and the inconvenience." As it happened, the restaurant manager for the wedding dinner had to hastily assemble two long tables to accommodate the FBI agents and their spouses and young children who had flown in from Oakland and, in some cases, from Washington, D.C.

"When all is said and done," summarizes Ethel, "we are a family. If something happens to one of our agents or one of our support people, we are there for them. Whether it's a baby born or a parent's death, the Bureau will wrap its arms around its employees."

SWAT Commander Craig Arnold, who retired in 2005 as the FBI's most decorated agent, echoes this sentiment, in somewhat more workaday terms: "In SWAT, we do it for each other, first and foremost—not for God and country, and not even for the Bureau—but for each other. When we bust through a door and walk into God knows what, our first concern is taking care of one another. And we feel we can do anything, because we get strength from each other."

Nowhere is the sense of brotherhood more palpable than at the funeral of a fallen FBI agent, which might be attended by thousands from the community and by hundreds of agents and law enforcement personnel. Assistant Director Tidwell recalls the sad duty of being the FBI's liaison to the family of his friend and fellow agent Mike Miller, killed in the line of duty.

"I helped plan the funeral," recalls Tidwell. "Several agents had offered to be pallbearers. But so had Mike's son, Mickey, who was only nine years old at the time. Frankly, I wasn't sure If he could handle the weight of the coffin. So I asked his uncle, who said he believed that Mickey could. So we did it that way. When we got to the grave site, we agents had all been very stoic, very controlled. But when Mickey helped lay his dad into the grave, he turned to me and gave me a nod. And suddenly . . . I couldn't be stoic any longer."

This sense of filial love, within all levels of the organization, is surely one of the most powerful motivators in the Bureau. It generates a desire to reciprocate and to be just as good a friend in need. Given such support—knowing that it was there for you all the time—would it even cross your mind to be unfaithful?

It should be noted, as a footnote, that the "competitors" of the FBI are often quite good at instilling loyalty, albeit a misbegotten kind. There are street gang members who would sooner die than betray their brothers in the organization. Many gang members remain loyal even when removed from all possible retaliation, and some have even "taken the rap" for a fellow gang member. Their very tattoos are celebrations of loyalty. Some organized crime members, as well, are similarly faithful; the loyalty of Mafia members who are willing to go to prison rather than "snitch" on their comrades is well documented. And the fanatic fidelity of terrorists, many of whom are quite willing to destroy themselves in a final blaze of "glory" rather than surrender, is self-evident.

Although we don't want to compare our business competitors to outlaws—at least not all of them—we have to recognize that their employees may be working for something beyond the paycheck. If ours are not, we will be at a disadvantage.

Why Fidelity Is an Issue in Free Enterprise

When a top performer leaves one company for another, and does so in a thoroughly professional manner and with proper notice and plenty of handshakes all around, management understands. After all, we're all adults here; the company had no "hold" on the employee. He or she had traded talent and skill for the compensation package and simply found something better. Perfectly understandable.

Why, then, are management's feelings hurt when a good employee leaves?

Deep down we all expect more than a fair trade of output and input—in both directions—between management and the employee. Although it will be unexpressed, the employer expects that the personal relationships developed at the company should mean something and should have added more dimension to the employment contract. Similar (and similarly unex-pressed) expectations are held by the employee; he or she feels entitled to be thought of as more than a unit of production. And, indeed, favors are granted by both parties all the time, as employees work a little "overtime" at no charge, and as manag-ers give an occasional afternoon off so the employee can attend to a personal affair. Most of us believe that "work should be about more than money," although it is probably management that believes it more fervently.

Generations ago, the employer was the stern patriarch for whom the employee worked her entire career. In the modern age of business, the concept of loyalty is something of an anach-ronism. Most professionals have a number of employers listed on their résumés, each company presumably a step above its predecessor in terms of the responsibilities assumed and the in-come earned. Loyalty was no doubt expected by each company, and it was given—at least up until the moment the employee knew she was going to jump ship. From that moment on, her loyalty was divided. Unless she had told her current employer of her intention to leave, the current employer had no idea of the conflict of interest experienced by the employee.

There is also in modern times the emphasis on loyalty to the self, drummed into every member of the workforce by family, friends, coworkers, and the popular culture. We are advised not to squander our loyalty on any organization. Our real duty, we are told, is to ourselves and to our own loved ones. After all, the company would not hesitate for a moment to fire us if condi-tions called for it, and worse yet, it would do so without notice, even though the layoffs might have been planned for months. We must keep things in perspective, we are told. The company we work for is simply a means to an end. For all its talk of being a family, the company is a locus of production; one's "brothers and sisters" can be fired at a moment's notice for not meeting or exceeding ever-increasing expectations set by a cool and calculating management that views the employee as a renewable resource. Why give one's loyalty to an organization that will exploit one's talents until one has no more to give? According to this line of reasoning, employee fidelity is nothing more than a variation of the Stockholm Syndrome.

For its part, management is much more dependent on employee fidelity than it would care to admit. Simple absenteeism—an indication, if excessive, of a lack of employee commitment—can cost a company plenty by year's end. Employee turnover, involuntary or voluntary, can represent expenses all out of proportion to the departing employee's salary. The process of finding and training a replacement can take months of downtime. Not only can business be lost during this recovery period, but it can be taken away by the former employee, especially if he or she happened to be a top sales or customer service rep. Then there is the direct, intentional damage caused by disgruntled employees. Loss prevention experts claim that employee theft is in many industries responsible for more lost profits than any other market factor. Sometimes, we even hear of cases of outright employee sabotage.

But there are also subjective aspects to corporate infidelity that cannot be measured; indeed, the existence of some of these factors can scarcely be admitted to by a habitually optimistic manager. Some employees, for example, take a certain amount of pleasure in the failures of the very company they work for. Perhaps an employee doesn't like a particular manager who is pursuing a major customer contract. When the employee hears that the manager has failed to secure that piece of business, she is secretly gratified, even though her own future with that company could be negatively affected. No doubt that employee would be the manager's greatest fan if that contract meant the continued life of the organization—and therefore of her own job—but many in the company, not knowing the big picture, assume there are always many more contracts to be had.

The issue of envy must also be faced. Internal competition among all employees for but a few coveted managerial and executive positions creates hopes and aspirations that must be occasionally dashed. When the individual who won the competition later fails a high-profile assignment, the "loser" feels vindicated. And that kind of satisfaction, after the fact, comes very close to actually wishing failure on the victor from the first day of his or her promotion. This is a sad fact of business life; behind the smiles and the handshakes and the pats on the back is an active voodoo at work, emanating from the unlikeliest of individuals.

Finally it must be realized that there is a slight antipathy on the part of all employees toward the organization simply for the necessity of having to work for a living. Grateful as we are for a steady job, there is something in all of us that resents the very need to work, which subconsciously blames the company for the alarm clock going off at ungodly hours, the traffic jams along the commute, the security lines at airports during our business trips. It is irrational and silly—and certainly less insidious than co-worker envy or the secret desire to see one's manager or executive fail—but this suppressed resentment toward the organization for being an organization in which we must labor must be recognized.

Engendering fidelity toward the organization in free enterprise is a major management challenge, all the more so because companies have no right to expect it in the face of a lucrative and unmatchable competitive offer.

Or do they?

There are examples of organizations that inspire loyalty

without paying for it. Colleges, judging by the deafening level of enthusiasm at football and basketball games, do a pretty good job of inculcating fidelity in their students. Hoary bronze busts on campus are polished by the countless pats of generations of students wishing for the good luck a touch will impart. Ivy-covered walls and silver-haired professors in flowing gowns add to the majesty of age-old ceremonies attended by aging alumni and freshmen alike, creating that wonderful juxtaposition of generations in harmony. Decades later, former students will wipe away nostalgic tears at the memories of their college experience and sing the school song with voices quavering with emotion.

Isn't there just a little bit of irony in the fact that many old-line, tradition-rich companies, which have been *paying* their employees for decades instead of *demanding* tens of thousands of dollars of tuition annually, cannot seem to evoke similar devotion?

The same can be said of the loyalty engendered by military units, especially considering that their members have less in common socially than do most employees and stay together a much shorter period of time, then disperse back into civilian life in widely scattered regions of the country. Yet grown men will regard their now ill-fitting uniforms as sacred cloth and gaze in reverence at an intricate shoulder patch depicting the nearly mystical symbols of their former unit. And just try to persuade them to miss their thirty-year reunion! While their company, which pays them ten times more than the military ever did and treats them like human beings on top of it, cannot induce a kind word.

The comparison is admittedly a bit unfair. Soldiers live, train, and fight together, and lifelong friendships are forged by the intensity of the military experience, not by the comparatively brief duration of an enlistment. But the uniform, the patches, the "Semper Fi" bumper stickers, the "Go Navy" coffee mugs, and the air squadron wall plaques collected by many veterans go beyond the buddy experience. The veteran is also pointing with pride (and sometimes irreverent pride) to the organization he or she served. The military, for all its heavy-handedness, successfully creates a sense of common cause at one time in the veteran's life, and it is not forgotten.

Charitable organizations offer perhaps the best example of how to win the hearts and minds of the rank and file without paying for it. A volunteer thinks nothing of spending precious weekend time, and evenings after a long day's work, in service of an organization that in turn serves a cause he or she believes in. A cancer survivor, or a person who has lost a loved one to the disease, is motivated to give time to the Cancer Society for personal reasons. But the lives of many Cancer Society volunteers have not been touched by the disease, just as there are volunteer workers for world hunger organizations who have never themselves gone hungry. Yet these organizations are able to elicit a tremendous sacrifice—hours that would have been considered overtime if the volunteers had spent their Saturday at the office instead of in the service of their favorite charity. The retired volunteer could have spent his or her time on the golf course.

So it can be done. "Fidelity" is not necessarily associated with money.

The soft art of winning the bona fides of the workforce begins with a sympathetic management style that warrants reciprocity from the rank and file. To expect fidelity, management must be faithful to its people. All of us have probably had an individual manager whose demeanor made us want to go the extra mile, but for management across the board to elicit fidelity, the CEO must set the example. The personal leadership style of the chief executive can either win—or harden—the hearts of her employees. If the CEO is of a taciturn nature, she had best remain sequestered in her office. But a smiling leader who radiates confidence in the future, who pauses to chat with introverted employees, and who heartily congratulates the deserving for a job well done no matter how small the accomplishment can have a galvanizing effect on the entire organization. Even if her contact is limited to comparatively few individuals, her management style will be emulated by the junior execs and managers all the way down the line.

When that radiant personality publicly associates herself with the fate of the company, the employee will respond with extra effort. History has shown that the leader who fights, like Alexander the Great, "shoulder to shoulder" with his or her comrades will elicit nearly fanatical devotion. But the fact is the CEO is rarely seen by the workforce as someone prepared to "do or die" with the rest of the rank and file. On the contrary, the chief executive is regarded by most as a transient figure brought in by the board of directors, who will eventually jump ship to lead another organization—perhaps even a competitor—to success, whether the current company does well or not. In fact, the better the performance of the CEO, the more likely he or she is to use the current company as a stepping-stone to an even more extravagant salary. Employees love winners, but they may not bond with even the most charismatic CEO if all that charisma is directed toward reputation building rather than company building.

The Organization Must Match the Charismatic Manager in Charisma

The organization will always be at a disadvantage vis-à-vis the magnetic executive or manager, because it is difficult to be loyal to an abstraction. We put in the extra effort for the corporeal leader and for our flesh-and-blood managers, not for the company. This is why the loyalty of the employee is too often given just short of the organization's true goal—not to management, but to a particular manager. This is not good from the organization's point of view. Charismatic executives who leave their company often take "loyal" assistants with them; the fidelity of that assistant, although commendable, was fixed on a person, not on the company. Salespeople who have close relationships with their customers are often able to take those customers with them when they switch companies, much to the dismay of the previous employer, and here again the customer's loyalty was to the individual, not to the company he or she represented. Star employees sometimes jump to another organization and, nondisclosure agreements notwithstanding, reveal confidential information to the new employer. In this case, their loyalty was to a paycheck, not to an individual and certainly not to the company, and they will likely repeat the process during their unsteady careers.

While it is true that soldiers on the battlefield fight for each other instead of for the lofty ideals voiced by their generals, it is also true that if that is their only motivation, it represents a failure on the part of leadership. This is because the soldier needs both, as evidenced by the disturbing number of American POWs in North Korean prisons during the Korean War who, separated from their buddies, were unable to explain to their interrogators what they were fighting for and who rather quickly signed "confessions." Without the support of their fellow warriors, the "Army," as an abstraction, lost its sway. The same holds true for the corporate soldier: If the organization and its lofty ideals do not have an equal place in the heart of the employee, his or her efforts will be influenced unduly by peer presence and peer morale.

While they may be wonderful resources for the company,

the charismatic, superstar manager and salesperson must be recognized by the organization as competitors for the hearts and minds of the employees and of the customer. The CEO who communicates through a popular manager, who just seems to "connect" with the rank and file, does so at his or her own peril. The gaze of the rank and file must be lifted higher—higher, in fact, than even the CEO, who also may depart one fine day. It is the company itself that must abide in the hearts and minds of all employees.

To that end, senior management must unapologetically tout the achievements of the organization, in terms of the good it has done for its employees and for the public. Its history (to the degree it has a history) must be recounted and its useful future predicted—in terms compelling enough to enlist the long-term support of the employee. Most importantly, the organization must be cast in the light of an enabler. That is to say, the company should make it clear that its resources have helped make the good works of the individual possible. Where would FBI agents be, for example, without the Bureau? It is the Bureau that enables them to return kidnapped babies into the arms of their parents, to rescue terrified hostages, to prevent the wholesale murder of innocent civilians from a terrorist's weapon of mass destruction. The same can be said in less dramatic terms of most corporations and private companies, which provide the infrastructure for the production of vaccines; educational books; beautiful furniture; safer automobile tires; health care for the aged; cell phones that keep loved ones in touch; digital cameras that record beautiful memories; and the softest, fluffiest bathroom tissue on the market. Whatever the product or service, it is of use to somebody, and the company has made it available and will continue to serve the public with the loyal help of its employees.

This is not to suggest that money is of no value in cultivating fidelity. Few things warm the heart of even the most cynical employee more than a fat paycheck or performance bonus, but there are other loyalty-inspiring incentives. Many companies will pay a large percentage—or the entire price tag—of continuing education, such as an MBA program. When it does so, the employee feels as if the company has invested in him, and the employee wishes to repay its confidence. Company-sponsored 401(k) savings plans have helped many employees buy their first home. Although the employee is borrowing from himself, so to speak, the company has helped make the arrangement possible and therefore holds a "mortgage" on his affections. Certainly a major incentive would be continued health care for the employee after retirement, assuming he had remained with the company through thick and thin for the required number of years.

To carry this train of thought a bit further—to the end, actually—an organization with a history of long-serving, loyal employees might even want to consider a company cemetery for those associates and their spouses who have no particular resting place in mind. The idea is not quite as crazy as it no doubt sounds. Many people have not planned for their own deaths; the subject is so uncomfortable to consider that they continue to procrastinate. The company, by offering an alternative to commercial memorial parks, where they would be surrounded by "strangers," could relieve them of that responsibility.

Cultivating Bravery in the Workplace

On a sunny morning in Miami, April 11, 1986, a roving FBI bank robbery squad spotted the car of the two men they had been searching for, who were responsible for a series of deadly bank and armored car holdups. A felony car stop was initiated. The robbers suddenly jumped out of their car and started shooting with a pistol and a high-powered rifle. Two FBI agents went down, killed in action. Five more were wounded, among them Special Agent Ed Mireles. His right arm shattered by a rifle bullet, he managed to cycle his shotgun with his left hand, using the car bumper as a brace. After an intense firefight, the two robbers jumped into an empty FBI squad car and attempted to leave the scene. Agent Mireles, moments before passing out from loss of blood, staggered toward the car and fired with his left hand, killing both men.

Where does the FBI get such people?

Part of the answer surely lies in the recruiting process, which hopes to identify young men and women who are predisposed to rise to the challenge. An intensive training program follows, stressing, among other skills, firearms expertise and hand-to-hand combat techniques, both of which tend to foster the warrior spirit. But of most interest to the business community is the culture of courage the Bureau cultivates and maintains.

Every FBI field office across the nation has a permanent, and prominent, display of FBI service martyrs, agents who have been killed in the line of duty. These memorials not only honor the dead, but they serve to remind each living agent of the hazards of the profession. In the Los Angeles office, an entire lobby wall is dedicated, with photographs of each agent and a brief description of his or her heroism. The wall chosen for the display is nearest the lobby door; one can't help but be confronted by it. The eyes of the fallen heroes seem to greet the agent in the morning and follow the agent at day's end. The effect on the citizen visitor is awe inspiring; one wants to say a prayer. It is unlikely that the agents who pass by that memorial so many times each day, month after month, grow so accustomed to its presence that they no longer occasionally get goose bumps.

In addition to the permanent display are annual public ceremonies to commemorate the fallen heroes, so that their names and deeds are not allowed to pass from institutional (and public) memory. Average citizens who attend cannot help but be humbled by the sacrifices made on their behalf by agents in the prime of their lives. But the FBI agents who attend these moving ceremonies feel more than gratitude. They feel a spiritual obligation to continue the work of their predecessors, so that they will not have died in vain. In that respect, the annual memorial service—in a symbolic sense, a kind of funeral—is not only a somber tribute, but a powerful motivational event. The agent wishes to continue to be worthy of his or her credentials and to live up to the high standards set by heroes. Figuratively speaking, the day of an FBI memorial service is probably the worst possible time to rob a bank.

As in the military services, medals are awarded for bravery, and the awards ceremonies are taken very seriously in the FBI. (The unique manner in which the recipients are selected will be discussed later.) The Director takes as much pride in awarding a medal for valor as the agent does in receiving it—and as much as his or her family does in witnessing the event. Attached to a beautiful ribbon and miniaturized as a lapel pin that can be worn every day, medals offer an insight into the character of the recipient. One can tell at a glance that (a) the individual has been seriously challenged and that (b) he or she responded to that challenge with distinction. In that sense, medals are miniature biographical statements, worn with pride and recognized and admired by all within the organization.

The Need for Courage in the Workplace

While the attribute of personal courage is clearly required for an FBI agent, its need in the comparatively peaceful business environment is less obvious. But there are many times when we have to be brave at work—you may not be in grave danger as often as an FBI agent, certainly, but you need to be brave nonetheless. It takes courage to make a sales "cold call" or to call on an intimidating customer who likes to eat salespeople for breakfast. It's not easy for a customer service rep to face the wrath of a particularly upset customer. One must be brave to speak before a large group of customers or to confront the news media when it has its knives out for the company. A great deal of courage is required to turn in a thieving associate or to make an end run around a recalcitrant manager all the way to the CEO. And it takes guts to leave one's comfort zone and enter uncharted waters, as an individual and as a company. It takes courage to ask for a raise or for a promotion. Some days, it takes a bit of courage to wake up and go to work rather than call in sick.

Since courage is required in the workplace, it is the responsibility of management to cultivate courage, like any other workplace skill. There are a number of programs offered by consulting companies—such as corporate boot camps, white-water rafting trips, and even wilderness survival experiences—that are designed to put the employee into situations where he must rise above himself. The problem with these creative and vigorous exercises is (a) they are team oriented, (b) the courage one is supposed to develop is not readily transferable to business situations, and (c) they exclude older or disabled employees.

With all due respect to the quite proper emphasis on team building in corporate America today, the team environment is not fertile ground for the cultivation of *personal* courage. That's because there are always leaders in a group to whom the others will naturally look to and follow instead of becoming leaders themselves. Even when the employee is forced into a leadership position, the resourceful members of the group will bail him or her out. There is, of course, such a thing as team courage, and the shared experience can be quite invigorating for all concerned. But the effects are short-lived for the timid who find themselves alone once again back in the workplace—and lonely after the camaraderie of the group experience.

Secondly, all these robust courage-building exercises involving a physical contest with the environment (for example, mountain climbing, running obstacle courses, white-water rafting) are not particularly applicable to the deadly quiet of the boardroom, or to the confines of the customer's office, or to the speaker's podium in front of an audience whose attention has not yet been seized. Suddenly the team exercise along the banks of the Colorado River seems completely irrelevant.

One exceptional way to cultivate individual courage is to eradicate the number one fear of civilized humanity—the fear of public speaking. Conquer that fear and all others shrink in significance. Guide a person to the point where he can stand before an audience and retain the presence of mind he has in his own living room, and the prospect of climbing Mount Everest will seem a trifle. When a person loses the fear of public speaking, he loses most irrational fear. The difficult customer feared by the rest of the sales force will be a step down—way down—from the audience the salesperson had spoken to the day before. Asking for a raise or promotion will be a piece of cake.

Public-speaking courage is transferable to all business challenges, and it is not team dependent. The process can be accomplished in baby steps through a planned program exposing the participant to ever-larger audiences. The premier public-speaking resource is also, happily, the cheapest. Toastmasters International is one of the undisputed leaders in business leadership development. Chapters abound where the newcomer is gently guided, speech after speech, toward excellence. Many companies in fact have in-house Toastmasters clubs, where executives, managers, supervisors, and members of the rank and file are on an equal footing.

These in-house clubs are spawning grounds for future company leaders. Part of Toastmasters training is learning the art of giving constructive evaluations of each other's speeches. That means a middle manager may find himself in the position of suggesting to the executive vice president that she has to work on her eye contact, or on her body language, to become a better communicator. This clearly can be a tongue-biting experience. But for feedback to be effective, it must be given freely, in an open, trusting atmosphere. The very format of the company in-house Toastmasters meeting provides, therefore, unique opportunities to relate to one's superior on a peer-to-peer basis. The executives and managers, in turn, have an opportunity to witness a subordinate take control of a meeting and communicate effectively to the group. This is an incredible opportunity to audition. An employee can work at a company for forty years and never be seen in such a positive light, but in a Toastmasters club it happens every week!

The company club chapter also offers the courage-building advantage of an audience of peers. Nothing is as rattling as speaking before one's associates—and one's bosses! Once mastered, this ability alone is a qualification for leadership. When you speak to people as peers for an extended period of time, they become peers; they haven't stepped down—you have stepped up.

It must be noted that there is one aspect to the cultivation of bravery that has long been overlooked: The employee must feel as if the company is worth fighting for. If the employee is "fighting" for a paycheck or a bonus, that may be of temporary use to the company, but the employee can pursue those goals at other organizations just as easily. Management must somehow make the company, in the employee's mind, something to be protected.

Of course, one of the most blatant methods is to associate the employee's self-interest with the continued well-being of the company through the issuance of stock, the theory being that once an employee is a part owner of the organization, it behooves him to go the extra mile to support and defend his investment. The problem is, every other credible organization offers similar stock-sharing programs. And perks, while appreciated, do not necessarily engender passionate loyalty. One of the most famous workplace sociological experiments of the 1950s demonstrated this. A group of factory workers agreed to participate in an evaluation of the effect of improved conditions on production. They were given an extra coffee break daily, and production went up. Music was piped into the work area, and production increased. More and more perks were added, each with a corresponding positive effect. Then one day all perks were removed and the workers retuned to their original "bare-bones" working environment—and production continued to increase! When interviewed, the employees revealed that the perks had nothing to do with their happier state of mind. It was the sense of involvement, of being engaged in an exciting endeavor, that motivated them.

In order for employees to feel protective toward their employers, they must be emotionally involved. FBI agents believe in the work of the Bureau. They witness the damage caused by criminal enterprises and by terrorists, and they see the good the

FBI accomplishes. And there are plenty of corporate missions that are similarly compelling. Nurses, teachers, researchers, social workers, firemen, etc. count themselves lucky to be working for organizations that not only are in sync with their personal values but that empower them to further those values.

But even a company making widgets can engender something akin to this level of emotional involvement through charitable and community outreach. Company-sponsored public service projects that require the participation of the rank and file are one of the surest ways to join hands and to join hearts.

There have been, over the years, tremendous examples of selfless corporate behavior, willingly assumed by employees whose hearts have been buoyed by the weekend and after-hours sacrifices they have made. Entire neighborhoods have been resurrected from flood and tornado damage, community parks have been built, billions of dollars have been raised for good causes—not by government agencies, but by the rank and file of major corporations that have put up the resources to make these miracles possible. And we hardly ever hear of these heroic actions.

For some reason, "tooting one's horn" over good deeds performed is considered unseemly. We have been led to believe that acts of kindness should be secretive, that no one should know. In fact, according to this morality, if we are confronted with the question, we should deny that we've done charitable acts and brusquely change the subject. Apparently, the only acceptable way for the secret to come out is through a third party, preferably after the death of the do-gooder so that he or she does not profit in life from the philanthropy.

What nonsense! Not only are companies that have done great things for their surrounding communities entitled to toot their horns, they have an obligation to tell their stakeholders, who have a right to know that the company has donated some of its resources to a good cause. Further, the company should broadcast what it has done in order to demonstrate to other organizations how they can contribute to their communities.

Pride in one's organization is a great courage builder. It makes us stand up for our companies in the face of criticism, and it inspires us to great deeds. When a corporate "culture of courage" is coupled with good works, the employee will be a happy warrior indeed.

Cultivating Integrity in the Workplace

When an FBI agent takes the stand in a courtroom to give evidence, even some highly paid defense attorneys, who have made an art form out of attacking the credibility of cops off the beat, walk softly; they dare not antagonize jurors who look at the agent with obvious respect and with perhaps a little bit of awe. In all likelihood, the members of the jury have never even seen an FBI agent before, and they like what they see, a clean-cut, nicely dressed, low-key professional. They like what they hear as well. The FBI agent, college educated—and often with a law or accounting degree—is generally more articulate than his or her brethren in other branches of law enforcement. The evidence delivered is notable for its painstaking accuracy, and it is obvious to all that the investigative procedures have been scrupulously followed. When the agent has dispassionately let the facts speak for themselves, there seems little the defense attorney can do in the way of shaking the very positive impression the FBI agent has left in the courtroom.

As a society, we believe in the integrity of FBI agents and in the veracity of the evidence they submit. We may not always have faith in the justice system that tries the case, but polls indicate that the vast majority of Americans hold the FBI in very high esteem. If it were a publicly traded company the "success" of which was measured by the number of investigations that led to convictions, we would buy FBI "stock" for our grandchildren.

But imagine what it would be like without that trust if, for example, society as a whole believed the FBI to be corrupt. All of its investigations would be suspect, all of its warnings to the public scoffed at, all of it agents held in contempt by the public. Worse yet, the cream of the crop of society would never apply to be FBI agents; only scoundrels would. Honest people in trouble or in danger would not appeal to the FBI for help for fear it would only exacerbate the situation. Nor would any citizen go out of his or her way to help the agency with tips. Clearly, if the FBI is to accomplish its mission—protecting the homeland—it requires the full faith of the American people.

That the agency has been able to retain this trust, from its employees and from the general public, is a tribute to the transparent decency of the organization. When Director Mueller wants to make an announcement or respond to a criticism, he does so in person rather than sending out a damage control spokesperson. When he appears on television, the public sees a pleasant face and hears a moderate voice answering questions to the degree to which they can be answered. When he reaches the point where for security reasons he cannot continue, Mueller is saying, in so many words, "Trust me." And the nation collectively nods its head in understanding and affirmation. The public realizes that it may have a right to know, but not always publicly. And if the FBI doesn't have the answer—just yet—the American public is forgiving. We do not expect omniscience, just professionalism. And there seems to be little doubt as to the professionalism of the Bureau. Who of us would like to be on the receiving end of an FBI investigation, for any infraction?

Not only does the public trust the FBI, so does the criminal who chooses to cooperate with the Bureau. Every time a "wise guy" on the street decides to "make a deal" with the FBI and testify against the criminal enterprise he serves, or become an FBI informant at the risk of his life, he is confident that the Bureau will keep its side of the bargain by protecting his identity or by enrolling him and his family in the Witness Protection Program. And those expectations are based on a reputation of integrity, even in the underworld.

Here again, it all begins with the recruiting and training process.

"We try to hire people," explains Special Agent Jeff Green, leadership instructor at the Academy, "who share our core values, like accountability and leadership. From day one we talk about what it means to be an FBI agent and how you live and work in a glass house, with the world watching. That means you might have to change the way you behave in private, and might have to look a little nicer than you normally would otherwise. We stress in every class 'doing the right thing.' We want our agents to know they are entering a culture of honesty."

His fellow leadership instructor, Special Agent Skip Robb, believes the training program to be the foundation of just about all future behavior. "This is where the corporate culture is passed on. I know we're all about keeping up with change in a changing world, but some things you don't want to change, like the core values that have made being an FBI agent an honor. I don't know of any greater honor in the world."

An agent is expected to live up to the high standards of the Bureau throughout his or her career. And the proof is in the pudding. The number of "bad apples" that have been found in the FBI during the past one hundred years, out of hundreds of thousands of personnel, is so small as to be statistically irrelevant. And when they are discovered, it is by fellow FBI agents, who do not know which is more egregious, violating the law or breaking the sacred trust of the organization.

Sarbanes-Oxley Does Not Guarantee—or Even Promote—Integrity

A corporation's integrity is critical to the continued support of its stakeholders, primarily its customers, employees, and shareholders. Congress, through the Sarbanes-Oxley Act (SOX), has attempted to legislate integrity by making it more difficult to lie, cheat, and steal. Now, under SOX, one must lie, cheat, and steal in triplicate, which of course increases the chances of being caught.

If one looks at the impact of SOX legislation from a distance, perhaps from the vantage point of a foreign businessperson, it might seem unfair to burden all publicly owned companies for the fraudulent behavior of a handful. Less than a dozen companies, out of the some thirteen thousand listed on the exchanges, have made the news for having dishonest leadership. So now the vast majority of honest companies must continuously prove their innocence by keeping track of every activity in triplicate—on paper!—in the digital age when the need for cutting down trees is supposed to have lessened. Just as every single American must now prove, because of the actions of a handful of terrorists on 9/11, that he or she is not a terrorist before boarding a plane, every business leader of a public company must now demonstrate, through burdensome reporting requirements, that he or she is not a crook.

But requiring the CEO to personally attest to the accuracy of the company's financial reports, on pain of up to twenty years in prison and up to five million dollars in personal fines, does not alter the fact that there is such a thing as the division of labor. One cannot be a CEO and, at the same time, be a CFO, an accountant, a controller, a CIO, and the dozen other department heads that contribute to the financial report. Every hour the CEO must spend checking up on those who have been hired to do their jobs takes him or her away from the job of leading the company. The CEO must depend on the honesty of others because there is no practical alternative; the CEO cannot be all things to the company and still be a CEO.

Forcing the CEO to be liable for the work of his or her subordinates—work that is outside the area of the CEO's expertise and the accuracy of which cannot be checked down to the last penny without employing other subordinates whom the CEO must also be responsible for—does not guarantee integrity. It does not even promote integrity; it simply promotes compliance. The onset of SOX in all probability means that the CEO of the near future will have a strong legal, financial, or accounting background, not necessarily the best preparation for leading an organization to victory. The once visionary CEO now has put on bifocals. This is why it is silly to believe SOX discourages cronyism. In fact it encourages cronyism because the CEO needs to hire people he or she can trust implicitly.

But even the new breed of CEO may have some difficulty squaring the demand to maintain integrity with the demand for performance. "Performance" is the Prime Directive on every starship in the business universe. There is, of course, the obligatory published caveat: One's performance must never be sullied by violation of the company's ethical policies. Each employee is assumed to understand these ethical policies, because HR has required signatures attesting that the employee has read and has comprehended the noble standards of behavior expected of him or her. The piece of paper is then put into the personnel file in the event the employee ever violates these standards, so that the company can say, in effect, "You signed it; you were aware of our policy."

Just as police inspector Claude Rains was "shocked, shocked!" that gambling was going on at Humphrey Bogart's *Casablanca* nightclub, senior managers profess surprise and indignation should an overzealous salesperson be caught stretching the truth to meet the do-or-die sales quota they themselves have assigned. Now that a major customer is angry, the integrity of the company is at stake. The truth is, it always was.

The scandals at Enron, Tyco, WorldCom, et al. have given the public the impression that personal greed is the greatest threat to the integrity of a company. But it is probably much closer to the truth to suggest that the executives and managers who push the ethical limits of their organizations do not do so for personal gain other than to keep their jobs. They push the limits to meet the expectations of the shareholders.

The pressure to perform on a quarter-to-quarter basis keeps even the CEO on a short leash. Every quarter he or she must meet the expectations of shareholders who for the most part do not harbor a long-term view of the company. Indeed, the majority of shareholders may not know the industry well enough to be able to even formulate a long-term vision for the company. Their attention is focused not on the industry or on the company per se, but on tracking the price of the stock as it moves up and down the various market charts. Should the stock price plummet or fail to rise—often because of market forces that have nothing to do with the quality of leadership within the company—the shareholders may demand that the board of directors makes changes.

It is arguable that shareholders are not particularly concerned about integrity with a capital "I." Why should they be? They're not in it for the long run themselves, and they don't expect the CEO to stay around forever. It is true they do not want a corporate scandal and the resulting drop in share value, but it must be remembered that the Enron shareholders were the biggest fans of the company's executive team up until the devastating revelations. So, apparently, was the board of directors.

When there is a corrupt company, the general public identifies the office of the CEO as the seat of corruption. And, indeed, whenever a major business scandal hits the papers, it always seems to involve the CEO. He or she is not believed to be a "bystander," but rather the initiator of the unethical behavior, just as the juries decided in the cases of Enron, WorldCom, and Tyco. It just doesn't seem credible to the man in the street that the bank president can be unaware of the fraud perpetrated under his or her very nose or that the presidential candidate can be so out of touch as to profess surprise and dismay at the unscrupulous actions of his or her campaign manager. We naturally hold the person at the top accountable, and if by chance he or she really wasn't aware of the shenanigans taking place, it is nearly an equally damaging indictment of his or her vigilance.

On the happier side of the issue, the CEO is also assumed to be the fount of integrity in an admirable, well-run organization. Since he or she is inexorably associated with the integrity of the company in the minds of the general public, the employees, and the investors, it falls to the CEO to maintain and cultivate the integrity of the organization—even though his or her tenure in that post may be uncertain. Appointing a senior executive as ethics officer is a fine idea, but integrity cannot be delegated. It is primarily an issue of leadership, not enforcement. It is the CEO's duty to personify and to cultivate honor wherever he or she walks—like Robert Mueller, for example, does. Leaders must never forget that the eyes of the company are always upon them. The executive team, middle managers, supervisors, and the rank and file are always observing, looking for confidence, certainty, and decency. When the CEO's personal conduct is out of sync with the stated corporate mission, an implicit message has been sent to the hardworking faithful throughout the organization, and in some cases it is a slap in the face.

The clearest sign of a leader who really cares about the unsullied reputation of the company is a zero tolerance policy toward ethical violations, without exceptions or extenuating circumstances. No breach of the policy can be considered too small to punish, because "baby steps" inexorably lead to ever more confident attempts to get away with something. Virtually all major cases of corporate crime, or any crime, for that matter, have a trail of graduated offenses, each one emboldening the perpetrator. A zero tolerance policy recognizes this fact and nips the process in the bud—at least at that particular organization (the violator may misbehave elsewhere). It also relieves the CEO from being put in the position of an appellate judge. The CEO can claim, with justification, that his or her "hands are tied" by the zero tolerance policy; it cannot be overridden. There will be no agonizing over decisions; the policy, like a physical law of nature, is implacable. Once the word gets around the organization that ethical breaches will not be tolerated, employees so predisposed will think twice, maybe thrice, before violating company policy.

CHAPTER THREE

Managing Readiness

The importance of simulation in the workplace • Cultivate a "one for all, all for one" corporate culture • Win with the tools you have, not the ones you wish you had • Manage failure • Develop the habit of visualization • Ask for a plan!

> I'm always running scenarios through my head of things happening unexpectedly, and asking myself "What would I do?" It's a habit. I do it all the time, every day.
> —STEVE MARTINEZ, SPECIAL AGENT IN CHARGE, LAS VEGAS OFFICE

In business journals we read stories of companies being "blind-sided" by the competition, or being caught "flat-footed" by un-foreseen market forces, or "looking the other way" when they should have seen "the handwriting on the wall." If a business is "caught napping" by a significant challenge from the market-place, the very worst that can happen is bankruptcy—which is bad enough, certainly. But if the FBI is blindsided and unable to detect and disrupt a horrific terrorist attack (for instance, with

67

a weapon of mass destruction), it is not an exaggeration to suggest that millions could die. How the Bureau maintains its state of readiness, then, will be of interest to all of us who face the less severe penalty for not being ready.

The Importance of Simulation in the Workplace

On April 4, 2005, dozens of FBI agents in the New Haven, Connecticut, and Newark, New Jersey, field offices were suddenly called upon to drop whatever they were doing and race to two separate crisis scenes. A chemical bomb had exploded in southern Connecticut, injuring hundreds attending a waterfront festival and imperiling the city with poisonous fumes. Simultaneously, authorities had reported a biological attack on the campus of a New Jersey university; pneumonic plague toxins were spewing out of a hose nozzle protruding from the window of a van parked near a dormitory. That the attacks were part of an orchestrated terror campaign soon became clear. One of the five suspects arrested in the New Jersey plot unwittingly provided information leading to the arrest of another three accomplices in Connecticut. At the end of the day, more than six hundred FBI employees—agents, analysts, victim specialists, evidence experts, and SWAT and crisis response professionals from adjoining cities and states—had been thrown into the investigation.

It was only a drill.

FBI agents put in long hours, and even when they're "through for the day," they're not. Agents are on call twenty-four/seven, and well-deserved deep sleeps are frequently interrupted. Since surveillance operations—the trademark of FBI investigations—can take months, agents frequently spell each other on overnight watches *after* working all day and usually juggling three or more investigations at a time. Wedding anniversaries are forgotten, soccer games are missed, and family dinners with all at the table can become increasingly rare events.

You would think that with all the hours in the day already maximized, the Bureau wouldn't want to stress its agents any further.

Yet suddenly and without warning, every agent in the field office may be required to drop whatever he or she is doing and participate in a prolonged and realistic exercise (bomb threat, hostage situation, kidnapping, terrorist attack, etc.) dreamed up by their managers, who are themselves overworked!

Management would not call for these time-consuming exercises, which take agents away from their vital tasks, if it didn't believe in the power of simulation. The continual implementation of realistic simulation exercises is, in fact, one of the reasons FBI agents can react quickly to the unexpected. When "battle stations" sound, management and the rank and file participate wholeheartedly, as if the lives of American citizens depended upon their actions. Often involving national and even global coordination, these drills are treated as if they were the real thing.

But the FBI's penchant for ongoing realistic simulation exercises does not, at first, cry out to be implemented in the business world. As businesspeople, we tend to regard "drills" as something to be done early in our careers with the company—in the training room—in order to prepare for the "real thing." Once we graduate from our training and are loosed into the competitive marketplace, we are forever engaged in the real thing, called "making a living." We no longer have the luxury of being able to hold practice sessions. We are already in the struggle, tooth and nail.

While most CEOs would heartily agree that "practice makes perfect," that particular truism appears many notches below "time is money!" on the corporate list of venerable adages. Drills, if they are to be realistic, are expensive and time-consuming, requiring the assistance of the whole corporate support structure. "Why," stammers the indignant controller, "you might as well shut the company down for a day!"

Realistic drills, then, are usually relegated to the occasions when a cadre of employees has gathered together for a general purpose, such as an annual sales meeting. In the midst of classes, pep talks, and vendor show-and-tell, there might be a group project designed to help the salespeople when they return to the field. While certainly better than no drill at all, these kinds of simulation exercise tend to be few and far between.

But realistic drilling is a very, very powerful tool. When the astronauts in the glorious days of the Apollo lunar program returned from the moon, their colorless remarks seemed to disappoint the media. "It was just like the drills we had done a thousand times before," was the most common reply to the breathless question, "What was it like to land on the moon?" The interesting point is, up until their first landing, the astronauts were "experts" in something they had never actually done. They had never done it for real, but they knew how to do it through repeated simulation.

The U.S. Navy's Top Gun pilots are recognized as the best jet fighters in the world, even though they may have never been in combat. Martial artists who have never been in an actual back-alley fight are nonetheless "veterans" of countless sparring matches in the dojo. How would "the real thing" differ? Would the attacker use a knife? That contingency is practiced again and again. Would the attacker be really angry? That too is simulated on the mat. Airline pilots, through realistic drills in the cockpit simulator, become expert in emergency maneuvers they have never actually performed—and hope never to perform—in real life. So important is their performance in the simulator that mistakes while "practicing" can be career ending. Actors go through grueling rehearsals before opening night and consistently claim that "the more grueling the rehearsal, the easier the opening night." Why should the business profession be any different? Are our challenges so easily met that frequent, realistic practice is unnecessary?

Many authorities have pointed out that our subconscious mind is unable to differentiate between simulation and the real thing. But is that quite true? It's very possible that it can differentiate and that the simulated exercise is worse than the real thing. How many of us would be relieved to hear that our required "practice" presentation before top management has been canceled? The jitters we felt up until that moment were real enough. Ask any salesperson if she's more nervous over the prospect of delivering a presentation before her fellow salespeople or before the actual customer. More often than not it is the "practice" presentation before one's peers that is most feared. That's because the coworkers know the salesperson and the product much better than the customer does. The differences would be similar if we were to give an actual presentation before strangers or a practice presentation before the spouse and the in-laws. Give us the strangers!

But "being ready" implies being ready for anything. When FBI management calls for a drill, the agents participating are hard pressed to predict what will be thrown at them. Anything can happen. Management knows that confidence built upon anticipation of an experience similar to the one practiced can be easily shaken during "the real thing" if something goes awry. *The New Yorker* once featured a cartoon of a stage director "rehearsing" coughs and sneezes on the part of a simulated audience to inure his actors to the distraction. It would be wise to include similar possibilities during the simulation—perhaps a hostile customer, or a product question completely out of left field, or the sudden failure of the audiovisual system—all of which could easily happen in real life. After every drill, it would be wise to do what the FBI does: debrief all participants (see Chapter 7) for their reactions and their honest self-evaluations. We all learn through our mistakes, and mistakes are certainly better made during a drill rather than during the real thing.

So many wonderful things happen during a simulation exercise it is a wonder they aren't practiced more frequently. Realistic practice sessions afford us the opportunity to see it "done right" by people we might want to emulate. Drills are especially important for the sales department. Not only do salespeople overcome fear and gain confidence, they also build relationships on the sales team and within the support structure of the company. They learn whom they can go to for help and whom they want to ride into battle with—all because of a drill! When the drills are conducted holistically, with all departments in pursuit of a common goal (see Chapter 7), everyone benefits.

It should not be overlooked that the FBI drills because its competition also drills. The terrorist "pilots" on 9/11 had never flown a 757 before; they learned in cockpit simulators. Gangs of thieves have been known to build realistic mock-ups with which to rehearse their respective roles in a major robbery. Foreign spies have been through countless hours of simulation to prepare them for the characters they will assume on American soil. In the far more tame business world, many of our competitors also prepare diligently to win the contracts we covet. On the assumption that everything else being equal "he who prepares wins," we should do likewise.

If the simulation is sufficiently, perhaps even frighteningly, true to life, then the "real thing" will be a step down, not up.

Cultivate a "One for All, All for One" Corporate Culture

Nothing hurts organizational readiness more than competitive squabbling between disparate corporate subcultures and fiefdoms that have differing and sometimes even antagonistic agendas. The FBI, by the very nature of its work and by the quite necessary division of labor, would seem to be fertile ground for the development of subcultures. In fact it seems positively fertilized! Agents work in highly specialized and tightly knit squads, specializing in counterterrorism, counterintelligence, cyber crime, public corruption, gangs, fugitive apprehension, forensics, drugs, securities fraud, and other esoteric niches. Walking through an FBI field office, one sees clean-shaven men in three-piece suits, bearded ruffians in hooded sweatshirts, women dressed in business attire and in gang colors—agents all. The squad members share risk, eat lunch, and socialize together. Each agent no doubt thinks his or her squad is engaged in the most important work in the Bureau, and as a manager you would want them to think that way to be effective. You would also want each squad to be highly motivated, proud of its own heritage, mission oriented, and—being closest to the task—self-managed.

To further complicate matters, a squad's work is of a confidential nature. While restricted information is no doubt readily shared, under the new paradigm, from department to division and from the Bureau to other national security agencies, it is still not the kind of information that can be casually discussed or inquired about. And it is a fact of organizational life that confidential knowledge shared by a group tends to strengthen the bonds of mutual trust. Firemen, for example, form tightly knit teams, but firemen do not deal with top secret restricted information. Take that cheerful band of brothers and lay the burden of national security on their shoulders, and the hearty camaraderie might harden into tight-lipped suspicion of all outsiders— "outsiders" being a relative term applying to anyone outside the group.

Not only is the work highly specialized and confidential, it is frequently dangerous, further reinforcing the "I've got your back" ethos.

Given all these conditions, why isn't the Bureau plagued with subculturalism?

Robert Loosle, Special Agent in Charge (SAC) of the criminal division at the Los Angeles field office, couldn't have a more disparate cast of players to direct. "We have squads of agents working on white-collar crime, public corruption, bank fraud, and other squads working to take down gangs, criminal enterprises, bank robbers, serial killers, kidnappers, etc. But it all fits together. The violent crime agents very often have to come to the 'paper-pushing' accountants or cyber experts for help. Because there's a lot of crossover, with the intricate ways in which money is laundered, or the ways enterprises communicate or get funding. So the managers here are always showing everybody how important they are to the final resolution of a case."

Loosle believes in having awards ceremonies open to everyone in the office. "Then, in front of everybody, I will tell the story behind the awards, and make it clear how each person being recognized contributed to the overall success of the mission. Nobody expects an award for doing their job well, and most agents in all modesty would say it wasn't necessary. But even the most hard-boiled agent walks away a little taller than he walked in after one of those ceremonies. That's because we all like to be recognized in front of our peers—me included."

Loosle recalls a moment of confusion on the part of one recipient after one awards ceremony. "An agent who wasn't directly involved in the case walked up to me afterwards and asked why I had thanked him. He said, 'I didn't lift a finger on that case.' But he had, and just didn't realize it. He filled in, here at the office, and took up the slack for the lead agent who went out into the field. I wasn't being gratuitous. His presence here in the office really was important to the success of the mission. When I explained that to him, he understood and walked away with a grin on his face."

The cooperative ethic in the Los Angeles field office is palpable. "When another squad needs help," explains Loosle, "everybody here will momentarily drop what they're doing and pitch in." Sometimes that cooperation is expressed in manpower out on the street, sometimes in desk time, and sometimes simply in active listening between agents seeking to bounce ideas off their peers. "Older agents, of course, love to give advice, and the younger agents soak it up. But even experienced old hands will, if they're reaching a sticking point in an investigation, use their fellow agents as sounding boards. No matter how busy the agent is, he or she will give the benefit of their experience to another." And, of course, that makes sense. The Hollywood stereotype of the incommunicative veteran agent playing his cards close to the vest would probably not be a particularly successful investigator in real life, when information from oblique angles can be so critical to connecting the dots.

The FBI knows that unit solidarity, for all its benefits, can be counterproductive. The Bureau cannot afford to be an organization made up of disparate subcultures that over the years balkanize into miniagencies of their own. On the contrary, for the FBI to be successful it must maintain an open environment of mutual respect, common cause, and shared information. Communication between squads, between divisions, and between other agencies is everything. It may have been true during World War II that "loose lips sink ships," but in today's information-integrated environment, so can "tight lips."

Today's corporate environment is no less susceptible to the cultivation of subcultures. Various departments in a typical organization compete against each other for budget and resources every year. Employees tend to socialize within their own departments and often have no concept of the goals other departments are pursuing. Individuals vie against one another for promotion. Sad to say, one's associates are not always forthcoming with discreet, helpful advice—until the moment arrives when they can do so publicly, such as at an awards dinner, and be recognized for being so "helpful."

Not only is there internal competition for resources; some departments are actually at cross-purposes with each other. The sales department wants to sell a much desired software upgrade, whereas R&D wants to hold back its release until the software is perfected. Quality control has ideas for an even better manufacturing process, while the controller wants to cuts costs. Marketing pushes to move into uncharted territories and new product lines, while customer service wants to stick with its core expertise. Manufacturing wants to take advantage of serendipitous opportunities by stocking more inventory, while the CEO wants the "lean and mean" company to receive its supplies just in time. And often the competition is between the company and the shareholder, as senior execs resent postponing R&D or facility expansion expenditures to meet the quarterly numbers expected on Wall Street.

Further exacerbating the challenge of creating a "one for all, all for one" corporate culture is that management itself is a subculture. Managers eat lunch together, have closed-door meetings together, and seem to share a coded language of their own. Managers seem immune to the consequences of failure. While they are fond of saying they sit in the "hot seat," it's the rank and file that seems to sweat it out when layoffs are announced. Managers seem to always survive, like those resilient life forms that lived through the extinction event that killed off the dinosaurs. The rank and file sees what it perceives to be the invulnerability of the managerial "class" and is understandably suspicious and cynical of pep talks designed to spur team synergy.

Managers do not help their cause when they seem to play their role so ostentatiously. Upon promotion from the rank and file, the first thing a manager seems to do is disassociate himself from the rank and file. The newly donned starched white shirt is the very symbol of his estrangement from his past; he might as well wear white gloves. The newly promoted manager is so aware of his duty to be impartial that he seems aloof to his old buddies. And what has happened to his own view of management? A year ago he felt like an overworked and unappreciated "worker bee," and now he seems to think the worker bees don't do enough and need to be constantly prodded. And the Solomon-like judicial air he assumes when dispensing workplace justice is laughable.

How are managers who do not have the respect of their associates going to create a company-wide spirit of cooperation for the common good? All the impassioned "motivational" speeches, all the company newsletters praising this or that team, and even the awards ceremonies will be looked upon with cynicism.

On the other hand, managers who are seen to be sharing the mission—and the fate—of the rank and file will be revered. Awards from them will mean something. When Bob Loosle hands out awards, he is not reaching down from the clouds on Management Mountain, nor is he reaching up with the admiration of one who has never known the danger and hardships of this line of work. His handshake is peer to peer, and that's what makes the award meaningful. Perhaps the first step to creating an "all for one" corporate culture is to have a management team, from the top down, that the rank and file perceives as being in the same boat with them.

It must be remembered that sometimes in private enterprise it is not a matter of inspiring employees to work for the common good; it is a matter of *allowing* them to do so. Managers can be, for understandable reasons, tightfisted with their allocated resources. If an employee asks permission to help a counterpart at a different branch to overcome an obstacle, the manager may demur. The employee is making a noble gesture, but who is going to pay for the not insignificant travel and per diem expenses? Who will cover for the employee during his or her temporary absence? And who, when all is done, will receive credit for the resolution of the issue?

Retired undercover agent and hostage negotiator Tom Zyckowski worked for a number of supervisors during his twenty-five-year career with the Bureau (most of it spent in the Newark, New Jersey, field office). One supervisor in particular, Jim Darcy, never failed to impress his squad with his overarching vision. "His philosophy was 'It's the *Federal* Bureau of Investigation—not the *Newark* Bureau of Investigation,'" explains Tom. "Jim would share manpower on a widespread investigation involving other branches and was never concerned that his own squad might not get official credit."

Given the need for specialization, subcultures may be inevitable in private industry, but "subculturalism" is not. The FBI, in the strictest sense of the definition, undeniably has subcultures. Rob Grant, the SAC of the large Chicago field office, can say with a smile, "If you sit in on an organized crime squad, and then go visit a counterterrorism squad, it's like going from one world to another. It's a different mind-set, it's a different approach, it's a different culture, and it's a different kind of person. In some organizations that might be a problem. In the FBI, these subcultures contribute—each in its own unique way—to getting the job done."

Much of that desire to contribute is due to the unique calling of the profession, and the deadly challenges confronted by the organization. But the role of an "embedded" management team with a holistic organizational vision cannot be underestimated.

Win with the Tools You Have, Not the Ones You Wish You Had

A real-life FBI agent watching a Hollywood suspense movie must shake his head in wonder at all the gizmos his profession is supposed to have. One of the resources most often referenced in films is the omniscient databank. With one keystroke at the supercomputer, an FBI agent will retrieve all the biographical details of a suspect—down to the name of his elementary school teacher. If only it were so easy in real life! By what means would an information system gather data on a terrorist who has never been fingerprinted or otherwise documented, and perhaps never even officially photographed? One of the reasons FBI investigations can take years is simply because it takes that long to acquire the most basic relevant information.

FBI agents are also depicted on screen as having unquestioned official powers to conduct impromptu surveillance operations. In reality, the FBI agent is much more constrained in his or her activities than the public might imagine. Every phone tap requires court approval, and it may come as a surprise that not all requests are simply rubber-stamped. Reams of documentation must be provided to the judge, who has been schooled in a judicial system written by the Founding Fathers—who were infuriated by the arbitrary search-and-seizure practices of the British. The process can take weeks, by which time the opportunity may well have passed. Even if the judge does allow a tap, it will be literally for one phone. If there is another phone in the house, that conversation cannot be eavesdropped. If the suspect switches to a cell phone, the agents cannot listen without yet another court approval. If the suspect drives to a different city, the agents must rush over to yet another judge for permission. And it's safe to say that not all judges are sympathetic to the FBI, as indicated by the number of legal challenges against the Patriot Act on the grounds that some of the eavesdropping practices allowed are in violation of the Foreign Intelligence Surveillance Act (FISA). In fact, at the time of this writing, the U.S. House of Representatives passed a bill, by a vote of 227 to 189, that would tighten legal oversight on the ability of intelligence agents to "listen in" on terror suspects through wiretaps.

The Hollywood stereotype of a two-fisted FBI agent throwing away the book and taking care of business "his way" is also laughable. Agents are acutely aware of the rules of evidence, and the slightest misstep on their part could result in a case being thrown out of court by a judge who would have no choice but to toss it out.

The FBI agent is also portrayed as having so much authority that he can walk into any situation, flash that imposing credential, and all doors will be opened, all resistance will crumble. But in real life, if a suspect refuses to talk to an FBI agent, as criminals are wont to do, he or she must be subpoenaed. Criminals are not unaware of the limits of the law. They often have, in fact, a more practical knowledge of the Bill of Rights than a freshman college student majoring in political science. And once their attorneys are brought in, the pace of an FBI investigation can slow to a crawl.

There are no doubt many tools the FBI agent would like to have in his or her bag, and although few agents would be so impolitic to say so—many restrictions they would prefer to have loosened, to liberate their efforts on the counterterrorism and counterintelligence front. But they have to win with the tools they have. Frankly, these constraints make the FBI's achievements all the more impressive.

What would society's reaction be if the FBI waited until it was fully and ideally equipped before it took action? Obviously, the public would want the FBI to take immediate action with whatever tools it had. CEOs feel similarly about their own managers and employees.

Every business has finite resources. There isn't a CEO, an owner, a manager, or an employee who hasn't wished for the latest and greatest in technology to help him or her better compete in the marketplace. And there are employees in every company who believe that certain goals will be unattainable until the resources to achieve them are provided by management. We have a tendency to look askance at our own capabilities and to simultaneously exaggerate those of our competitors. We also are apt to compare our own paltry equipment to what is now available in the marketplace, or soon will be available, and wonder how we will compete against such perfection. And sometimes we compare our own humble capabilities to what the prospective customer believes is possible today. We might even become so disenchanted with our company's limited resources that we wonder how we will ever recruit the best and the brightest from the nation's campuses.

There is, in fact, the spectacle of technology worship in today's business community. The demand for the newest software upgrades, and the willingness to wait in lines that wind around city blocks for the latest release of a new digital device, suggest that many people would feel ill equipped without these wonders. This obsession may be of trivial importance if limited to one's private life, but if a sales department, for example, feels ill-equipped to compete with its more sophisticated competitors, there is a problem. Because the salespeople must win with the tools they have, not with the tools they wish they had.

The lack of bells and whistles in a product line is a common excuse heard by sales managers from their field reps. "The customer wanted this functionality; the competition could do it and we couldn't." But there will always be things our competitor's product can do better than our own, and vice versa. If the desired functionality is critical to the customer's mission, then of course we bow out gracefully. But how often does the salesperson probe into the needs—or the perceived needs—of the customer? It could be that the "all important" functionality was a last-minute side benefit mentioned by the competition that has little present practical value to the customer. It could also be that our own product will soon have that particular feature but in the meantime can do many things better than the competitor's product.

Blaming the lack of proper tools for the loss of a contract can, of course, be legitimate, and the company may have to respond with the necessary investment. But even then, those improvements will take time to bring into being. Is the company supposed to opt out of the marketplace until it is ready to compete? This is definitely a management issue, because there will always be a reason to wait; there will always be a higher level of perfection to be attained; there will always be engineers obsessively tinkering to make their products better, even though they already exceed specs. Our ducks will never be in a row.

There is another sense in which the sales manager must not let his or her field reps become too enamored with technology, and that is in the art of presenting before a customer or group of customers. Multimedia presentations are visually impressive, but "virtual reality" is no match for the real thing, which is the human presence on the platform, corporeal, smiling, moving, and alert to the mood of the audience. Dependency on presentation technology is always a bit dangerous. Amazing and dynamic multimedia presentations have been known to "crash," bringing a moment of truth to the presenter, who has the option of endlessly fiddling with his laptop and projector before an audience that is rapidly losing interest, or of seizing control the old-fashioned way, by taking the stage and communicating with voice, eye contact, and body language. There is nothing more electrifying than a speaker who passionately believes in his or her product. There is nothing more persuasive than a human being who earnestly reaches out to the audience rather than standing in the shadows before an illuminated screen, clicking the next slide. Your salespeople should believe that *they* are the show, not the screen that displays a surrogate presentation.

Customers sitting in a darkened room with their eyes directed toward the light have an attention span that professional marketers know to be alarmingly brief. So the marketers, in an effort to recapture that lagging attention, respond with even more dynamics: zooming and retreating graphics accompanied by sound; off-center images that are supposed to engage the eyes of the viewer as he tries subconsciously to "draw" the image back to the center, where it "belongs"; and the "jitter cam," the incessantly moving field of view, a technique that is supposed to more effectively engage the eye. The net result is an audience bombarded into submission by sensory stimuli.

When customers, however, are asked to get out of the passive audience mode and come forward to "test-drive" the new product, they will become much more involved. Salespeople often dread this approach because of all the things that can go wrong. Without proper training in the product's functionality, the customers may create problems that would never occur in real life, and thus walk away from the presentation unconvinced. But those issues can be countered by a salesperson who knows her product like the back of her hand and who can take control of the learning situation. In fact, she will be forced to learn the product inside and out if denied the flash-bang presentation equipment.

Of course, "working with the tools you have" includes more than technological resources. Your salespeople may be intimidated by their competitor's larger customer service footprint, or by its unmatchable production capability, or by its ability to offer more favorable payment options. But if bigger and better always won the day, how can the startling successes of start-up companies be explained? There are countless examples of David beating Goliath in the domestic and global marketplace, and many more examples on the real battlefield, where outnumbered and ill-equipped troops have put their better-advantaged opponents to flight.

Salespeople who are intimidated by the size and capacity of their competition may be selling themselves short. Not all customers like to deal with huge conglomerates and would prefer to be "part of the family" of a smaller supplier. The customer may feel the smaller company wants his business more and will do more to keep it. He may feel the smaller company has a more focused core expertise compared to the larger conglomerate with a dozen divisions that are perfectly irrelevant to his own business needs. In fact, the sales managers at the larger companies may be giving their own people pep talks on how to overcome the Goliath image.

At any given point in time, a company has what it has and must try to win with it, not with a sense of resignation and not with a halfhearted attempt at a task one knows to be unachievable. Managers may have to occasionally give a modern-day rendition of the speech Shakespeare's King Henry V gave to his demoralized troops at the Battle of Agincourt. Hopelessly outnumbered by the French, the exhausted English were persuaded by their young warrior-king that they were *fortunate* no reinforcements could be expected, because their glory would not then be diminished. The soldiers were roused into believing that "we few, we happy few, we band of brothers" could win the day. And they did!

Six hundred years later, the modern manager must never underestimate the power of emotional appeal to his or her "troops." If, for example, the sales team quails at the prospect of going head-to-head against the industry's most prestigious competitor for a customer's order, they must be persuaded that their sales counterparts at the larger competitor are "order takers" who have never had to sell anything in their lives. The team must be reminded that their own company, though much smaller, is an elite corps of specialists. Why they should even feel a bit sorry for the larger competitor—for its inability to turn on a dime, for its impenetrable bureaucracy, for its massive overhead, for its vast infrastructure of separate business entities that barely know each other. Their own company, on the other hand, is quick to respond, nonbureaucratic, unburdened by overhead, and a family. The customer would be crazy to pick anyone else.

Manage Failure

In the aftermath of 9/11, outraged Americans turned to their government and demanded to know how the extensive planning required for the catastrophic attacks on the World Trade Center and the Pentagon—and for the intended attack on the White House—could have escaped the attention of the federal agencies charged with the responsibility of protecting the nation. The important work of the FBI and its long legacy of successes had been temporarily forgotten. Hardworking, earnest, and dedicated agents bore the brunt of public disapproval for the first time in their careers.

"We took it personally," reveals Assistant Director Stephen Tidwell. "After all, we had taken an oath to prevent something like that, and it happened. There was the almost instantaneous public perception that we failed—and failed absolutely."

Special Agent in Charge Rob Grant agrees: "The criticism hurt, there's no question about it. The agents who were affected the most were those with a shorter mind-set than the older veterans. There was anger, too, because of the appearance that some people in the intelligence community wanted to focus all the attention on the FBI when Al-Qaeda had been primarily an overseas, external threat. And at that time, it seemed as if there was no one publicly defending us. The Director was brand new. He had no choice but to accept the criticism and set about fixing the problem."

"It just seemed at the time," Grant concludes, "that there was nobody standing up for us, saying 'The FBI has served the nation well for a century. What it did do wrong it can fix.' Instead, all we heard was 'Why did you do this? Why did you do that?'"

What must have been doubly frustrating to the dedicated agents was that so little of the whole story had been revealed in the news, and the Bureau could not really make its case. It could not, for example, argue that certain communications between the CIA and the FBI had actually been forbidden by law; that Congress had been appealed to by the intelligence committee years earlier; and that the FBI had been tasked with domestic law enforcement, not global intelligence operations, and had done a pretty good job of it for a hundred years.

There was no question that the FBI's stock had fallen in the eyes of the general public, as indicated by highly critical (and uninformed) op-ed pieces, news commentaries, and public statements by elected representatives. And agents who had taken a pay cut to join the FBI and work fourteen-hour days fighting crime at the risk of their lives were suddenly less appreciated by the people they worked for—the taxpayers.

Dedicated FBI professionals or not, that is a management issue.

"It's hard to pump everybody up under those conditions," recalls Rob Grant, "other than to try to put everything in perspective. I'd remind my agents that they were exceptionally qualified and capable people and that in the long run we prove ourselves by the quality of our work."

"How successful have we been?" asks Stephen Tidwell. "We can't tell you all the details. What we can tell you is this: We haven't been hit again in six years."

In the business community, too, failure is a management issue, not so much in terms of how to punish failure but in terms of preventing the emotional reaction to failure today from detracting from performance tomorrow. As every manager knows, failure can become a mind-set. A series of failures can predispose an employee or a workforce to expect yet another.

Management knows this, yet it often unwittingly promotes failure by setting unreachable goals, on the theory that by aiming at the stars, one might at least hit the moon. This is the great irony inherent in high expectations: Often management does not really expect its goals to be met. A sales quota linked to a very attractive bonus, for example, is often set high enough to amount to a salary cap. Management does not expect to pay the bonus, and if for outrageously good performance it must, next year's goals will be doubled despite all evidence in the marketplace that the goal is impossible. The salesperson, of course, catches on quickly and begins looking for another company.

It is often said we learn from failure, and while that is certainly the case, we learn from success as well, but without the penalties. Management must realize that winning can become a habit, just like losing, and offer its people ample opportunity to achieve realistic goals.

But assuming the goals to be reasonably attainable, management has a problem on its hands if its employees dwell on having failed, or have been biased to fail again through poor performance, or have become risk averse. Just as we don't want the victorious to rest on their laurels, we don't want those who have failed to have long memories (other than remembering not to make a certain mistake again). Like Rob Grant, the manager must put failure in perspective and remind people of all the times their goals have been met and even exceeded. Most importantly, if and when the manager decides to forgive failure, he or she must also forget it and not use the employee's negative experience as a club in later conversations. Because failure fosters risk-averse behavior.

Matt Heron, chief of the organized crime section for the entire Bureau, makes it clear to his people that they should never become risk averse. "You have to encourage risk taking. You have to tell people not to be afraid to fail. Don't be afraid to try something creative, innovative. If you adopt a zero-defects mentality you are doomed to failure. I'm not talking about taking needless risks, but I do think it's important to be risk tolerant. If the reward at the end is greater than the risk you might be taking, then don't be afraid to study that risk and if it makes sense, to take a shot at it. I've never in my career criticized anyone for trying and failing."

Since the taxpayers are in the broadest possible sense the FBI's "boss," let us imagine the consequences of "our" agents becoming risk averse in response to the criticism we may have heaped upon them after a perceived failure. Suddenly our employees, the agents, would be loathe to make on-the-spot decisions. Seeking approval from above would become the preferred way to eliminate personal responsibility in case something went wrong. And, of course, that urge for "cover" would be felt at higher levels of management too. By the time somebody had the courage to make a command decision, the opportunity for swift action would have passed. It also goes without saying that in a risk-averse environment, entire avenues of investigation would seem fraught with the possibility of danger to one's career. Perhaps infiltrating an organization on a "hunch" could not be justified to a superior or would be seen by an oversight committee as a fishing expedition. And, in an effort to document one's every action, every suggestion, and every thought pro or con, the e-mails would be flying, with copies to everyone who might conceivably bear witness should the action ever be reviewed. Obviously, the effectiveness of such an organization would be drastically reduced. As citizen "owners" of the FBI, we do not—for our own safety—want our agents to be afraid to fail.

Certainly it is true in business that failure, if not properly managed, can lead to a risk-averse mind-set. But rather than "curing" the problem, management often responds by simply assigning the risk that the employee is reluctant to take, that is, by tasking an employee with a daunting goal. How he or she goes about meeting that goal, however, is a matter of attitude. If the employee doesn't feel "free to fail," the creativity necessary to successfully complete the task will be lacking. And one of the greatest business boons of all—serendipity—will no longer brighten the day of the CEO, because his or her people will no longer have the sense of abandon to follow their business instincts by walking into situations that just "feel" promising. They will no longer find themselves in the right place at the right time.

It should not be overlooked that failure can represent an opportunity to expand one's scope of work. It is unlikely that a person fails single-handedly. Often there have been aspects of his task that were out of his control, and perhaps he can seize control on the rationale that "if I'm going to be blamed for a portion of the scope of work that is out of my control, then put me in charge of that too." This is not unlike what happened to the FBI after 9/11. It was blamed in part for something out of its then current purview (global intelligence gathering). Now the Bureau has been given that responsibility, which is only fair if it is going to be held accountable for it.

Develop the Habit of Visualization

On September 5, 2006, forty-eight-year-old Steve Martinez waited patiently for his car to get through the car wash. As head of the Las Vegas FBI field office, he had just given a speech to an audience of retired agents and had stopped for gas on the way back to the office. As was his habit, he took in his surroundings at a glance. He nodded hello to fellow customers seated on the sunny patio and noticed, also, a couple of idlers who seemed to be "hangers-on" of the establishment. Through the gas station window he could see a woman playing video poker, a common sight in retail stores of all types in the city that never sleeps.

Moments later, the woman was no longer in sight; she

had gone to the restroom. His mind on the remaining appointments of the afternoon, Steve stretched in the warm sun and relived a satisfying bit of the speech he had just delivered. A bloodcurdling scream, accompanied by thudding noises, interrupted his thoughts. Just then, one of the male "hangers-on" he had noticed earlier burst out of the women's restroom.

In an instant, Steve drew his weapon and shouted, "Halt! FBI!"

The purse snatcher had no sensible option but to surrender. Steve ordered him to the ground, whipped out his handcuffs, and had him secured in an instant. With local law enforcement on the way, Steve realized not all the witnesses around him were smiling with admiration. Two or three guys, in fact, were obviously friends—and perhaps accomplices—of the man lying facedown on the street. They began to shuffle closer, protesting the innocence of their buddy. The woman, they insisted, had tried to rob *him*. Holstering his weapon, but with his hand resting on the grip, Steve made it clear through his authoritative voice, coiled body posture, and no-nonsense facial expression that it would be a big mistake for anyone to try to interfere with this arrest. The Las Vegas police arrived and, after seeing Steve's credentials, thanked him, with big grins, for taking care of business.

How long had it been since FBI executive Steve Martinez had pulled his weapon in an emergency and used his handcuffs? "It's been about fourteen years."

How long had it been since Steve had *visualized* pulling his weapon and using his handcuffs? "A couple of hours, maybe—if that."

Much has been written about the importance of visualization techniques in professional athletics and in goal setting of all kinds—as in "visualize the golf ball landing on the green," or "visualize yourself at your ideal weight." Many FBI agents have taken this technique and made it the habit of a lifetime. In a sense, many agents, and their counterparts in law enforcement, are "daydreamers." Only these daydreams are not particularly soothing.

"I'm always running scenarios through my head of things happening unexpectedly," reveals Steve Martinez, "like a robbery while I'm shopping in a store or standing in line at a bank, and I ask myself 'What would I do?' I really think visualization helps maintain a state of mental readiness. It's part of our training. Our instructors at the Academy used to pound into our heads, 'You'll do as you train.'"

Former SWAT Commander Craig Arnold, who retired as the FBI's most decorated agent in 2005, agrees wholeheartedly. "Visualization," he elaborates, "is such an important tool for mental preparation. We all practice this. When I'm driving home I'll visualize myself in various situations to cut down on the reaction time. Because, let's face it, the good guys are in the reaction business. It's the bad guys who initiate the force. The habit of visualization, and simulation exercises, can help you maintain a state of readiness, so that you react a lot quicker, with a thought-out, proper reaction."

The business applications of cultivating the habit of visualization are manifold and have been written about in many books, but the fine point is this: Through visualization we can make the imaginary experience much more intense than it will be in real life, and thereby render the actual experience innocuous. Before a sales call, for example, we can imagine being grilled relentlessly by the customer, with specific and shrewd questions about our product and service, the answers to which we say aloud in the car. Or we can imagine the customer raising objection after objection, giving us the reasons why he cannot make the purchasing decision at this time—and work out our responses as we drive. The technique is so powerful that we must keep perspective, lest we walk into the customer's office ready for bear when all he wants to do is give us an order.

Most of us do not like to consciously summon fear. Fear is an unpleasant sensation, and we have a tendency to evade or suppress thoughts that generate anxiety. We want to relax between appointments or on the commute home, listen to music, kick off our shoes, and let our mind wander where it will. The problem is, the anxiety is still there, buried alive, so to speak, and ready to leap up into our consciousness whenever we are confronted with a situation that evokes fear, such as a presentation before customers or an annual review with the boss—or, in the case of an FBI agent, a confrontation with an armed thug. By voluntarily facing our worst fears, we exorcise them. When the anxious situation appears, we have "been there, done that" in the theater of the mind, and we can fall back on the "experience." That's why thinking about the worst can be oddly relaxing. When fear is welcomed it dissipates because it has nowhere to go. And when fear is befriended, it is useful to us for the energy it gives us as it dissipates.

The habit of visualization promotes a state of readiness, so that we are not temporarily stunned by the unexpected in situations we have already anticipated in the imagination. Traditional martial artists have known this for generations. It may come as a surprise to learn that the beautiful solo routines practiced by karate students known as kata are movements in response to imaginary attacks. So too are the slow, graceful movements of tai chi (when accelerated into real time). The students who see kata or tai chi only as a series of movements never capture the realism of the exercise. In fact, there is an old saying: "When a student does kata, there is a gathering storm; when the instructor does kata, there is thunder; when a master does kata, there is *lightning.*" The difference in performance is related to the degree to which the practitioner visualizes the opponent's attack.

The state of readiness achieved by many FBI agents through the habit of visualization also makes them "ready" for the aftershock of concluded incidents. "Years ago, before we offered psychological counseling for law enforcement officers involved in a fatal shooting," recalls Craig Arnold, "statistics showed us that an officer who had taken a life in self-defense usually left the force within five years; it's that traumatic." The counselor who debriefed Craig after a shoot-out in which he was forced to take the life of a subject who had just shot a cooperating witness told him, "Your habit of visualization has prepared you for this and in some ways has immunized you from the aftershock of having killed somebody."

The great thing about visualization training is that it's free. No matter how drastically an organization's budget may be cut, mental "training" can continue in the imagination as we commute to and from the office or between appointments. Specificity is the key. The situations imagined must seem real—so real that the heart reacts, the palms get sweaty, and the hair rises on the back of the neck. Only then will the subconscious accept the scenario as an actual experience and tuck it away into the memory for instant retrieval.

Visualize Defeat Too, and Learn from the "Mistakes" You Made

One might think that Steve Martinez, being the director of his imaginary scenarios, always comes out ahead. But as often as not, he imagines himself defeated.

"Sometimes I'll imagine myself shot and lying on the street, and then I'll ask the same question, 'What do I do?' Because you can often do something as long as you're conscious—like agent Ed Mireles in that 1986 Miami gunfight."

One wonders what a psychologist might say to a person who frequently thinks about the worst that can possibly happen. In the modern era of positive thinking, we are cautioned to avoid negative thoughts and to cultivate a happy state of mind. Real life is already sufficiently grim, we are cautioned, so why accentuate the negative by dwelling on horrific possibilities?

But imagining defeat is definitely not "negative thinking" if, by doing so, one relives the mistake responsible, analyzes it in a kind of imaginary debriefing, and pledges not to make that same mistake again. To continue with the example of the sales call, it could be very productive to imagine losing the order and to imagine all the subsequent events such as telling your boss, your spouse, etc. Then, still in the theater of the mind, the reasons for the "lost" contract can be scrupulously examined. By walking into the actual, real-life situation, you have been given a second chance! The feeling of gratitude will be palpable, and the opportunity to redeem yourself will not be squandered.

No Matter How Well You Visualize, You Still Need the Equipment

The habit of visualization is only half effective if you cannot follow through in real life with the proper equipment. SAC Steve Martinez is in an executive position. One would expect him to be armed, of course, but as an executive he is no longer on the street slapping handcuffs on criminals and hasn't been in fourteen years. And yet he had his handcuffs on his belt at the car wash. Without them, the story could have had a different ending.

"When I was a new agent in El Paso, Texas," he explains, "we had an agent killed in the course of trying to arrest a bank robber. He had just been in line, like every other customer, when a guy walked in and robbed the bank. One of the reasons our agent was killed was that he didn't have his handcuffs with him. There's only so much you can do with a gun. Without handcuffs to control the subject, things can go south very quickly. You would probably have to fumble about with your belt to tie his hands, and in the process anything can happen, including being killed with your own weapon. I never forgot that case, especially because our office building here in Las Vegas is named after that agent, and I *always* carry my handcuffs."

To carry the example further, Steve could have visualized "slapping cuffs" on bad guys all he wanted, but the mental exercise would not have done him much good had the handcuffs been locked in his glove compartment in the middle of the car wash. He would have been compelled to use other, less dependable and less predictable means. Not only did he require the presence of the handcuffs on his hip, he had to be proficient with them. Since it had been fourteen years since his last official use of the handcuffs, he presumably had practiced with them in the interim, just as he frequently practices with his firearm (and is in fact required to qualify with the weapon every quarter).

Clearly, "being prepared" has a mental and a *material* aspect.

The subject of visualization deserves a footnote. While discussing the lifelong habit of mental preparation with FBI agents, the image of Inspector Clouseau unaccountably came to mind. In *The Pink Panther* and its sequels, the determined inspector gave standing orders to his loyal servant, Cato, to attack him whenever he least expected it, regardless of time, place, or pastime. And, of course, the ensuing scenes were all the more laughable because Cato's assaults came at the worst moments possible. Obviously, we must relax body, mind, and soul sometime.

"I'm not suggesting we do this twenty-four/seven," grins SWAT Commander Dale Monroe, "because we have lives, too. You have to have *some* balance."

Ask for a Plan!

A state of readiness presupposes a clear understanding of the communicated goal and the actions desired of a person. But the question remains: "Ready to do what?"

When an FBI supervisor parts company with one of his or her street agents after discussing an upcoming operation, the supervisor does not walk away wondering if "Jones gets it," nor does agent Jones ask himself, "What was it I'm supposed to do?" Both the supervisor and the agent are of one mind.

How do they know this? The supervisor has asked for a plan.

"There is an operations plan in place," explains Special Agent Jeff Green, "every single time we do something, with crystal-clear roles and responsibilities. That plan is then coupled with an after-action report upon completion of the operation. So you have a before and after record of what happened."

Even SWAT members, reacting to an emergency in which precious seconds count, draw up a plan. "While the hostage negotiations are going on, I'm getting my emergency assault plan in place," explains SWAT Commander Craig Arnold. "My supervisor is nearby in a mobile command post to approve the plan. Everybody is on the same page. The stakes are simply too high for us to have any doubt about that. A miscommunication can cost lives in this business."

It would be wonderful indeed to know that we are always "on the same page" with our associates as we cope with our less dramatic business challenges. Being of one mind with our boss or our team wouldn't necessarily assure success, but it would, at the very least, eliminate miscommunication as a reason for failure. And since poor communication is the cause of a great many failures large and small, that kind of certainty is worth pursuing.

But achieving clear communication is one of the greatest challenges in life, to say nothing of business life. Contrary to John Donne's eloquent observation "No man is an island," each of us is precisely that—an island, separated by a unique point of reference that cannot be simultaneously experienced by another because consciousness cannot be shared. Communication is so difficult, even under the most intimate of circumstances, that the lack of it is one of the most common causes of divorce or problems with our kids. When you really consider the obstacles to pure communication, it's a wonder we all stop at red lights.

Managers must ask themselves occasionally if they are doing more to discourage effective communication than to promote it. When the head of a department gives a presentation as if he is laying down the law, then concludes with a terse "Any questions?" those in the room may hear "Any objections?" instead. Soliciting questions after a presentation is, of course, important to effective communication, but it is all in the asking. If the presenter asks the question rhetorically—as if he does not want to be questioned, as if the words "Good, if there are no questions let's get to work" are already on his lips—anyone with the temerity to raise his or her hand will be met with impatience. Depending on the tone of voice, "Any questions?" can also be interpreted by the audience as "Have I made myself clear?" If so, few in the room will want to suggest with their question that the manager was anything but crystal clear in his presentation.

Communication can really suffer during an emergency, especially if the manager allows herself to become caught up in events. In an emergency, everyone looks to, and at, the manager. If her facial expression and body language express urgency, her subordinates will want to show, through similar body language, that they understand the situation. Soon everybody is wide-eyed and "ready for action," but very possibly without a clear idea of what to do. The urgency of the situation has been communicated, but not the remedy.

Of course, it takes two to tango. All parties must actually want to communicate, and this is not always a given.

A manager new to his assignment, for example, may be unsure of himself. He may be threatened by the prospect of a meaningful one-on-one conversation with an experienced subordinate or by a group meeting in which he may have to field questions he cannot confidently answer. Reluctant to give feedback, he may not even want to receive it for fear of being unable to respond intelligently

The subordinate may also be equally reluctant to communicate. We have all been in positions where a substantive conversation is the last thing we want, simply because we are not up to speed with the topic. We fully intend to fill that gap in knowledge as soon as we leave the manager's office, but for the moment we are relieved if the manager simply assumes that we are following the conversation. At times like these we pray for an uncommunicative manager. And in any case some of us are extremely shy in front of management and lose presence of mind with each step into the manager's office. We may nod our heads affirmatively, but our minds are clouded with self-consciousness. And we walk away wondering what exactly our boss was asking us to do. Too bad our boss didn't ask us for a plan. We might have averted a major mistake.

Asking an employee for a brief written description of his or her intentions is the surest practical way to know with certainty that the mission and the goal have been comprehended. It is also the surest way to know if you, the manager, are communicating effectively. Writing a plan allows the employee to step away from the spotlight of attention and to gather her thoughts. She has a chance to think about her approach before she takes that first step, or misstep. Knowing her manager will soon be reading and evaluating her plan, the employee will put herself in the place of her manager and ask herself, "What will *he* think of this?" That in itself is a worthwhile exercise, because by imagining herself as a manager, the employee's perspective widens. And, of course, once the manager has his subordinate's plan, he can offer a suggestion or two, in the form of questions like, "Have you considered this possibility?"

Being required to write a simple plan of attack forces us to strategize before rushing in where angels fear to tread. At that higher "altitude" we begin to see the possible consequences of our actions for others in the organization and for the customer. Another virtue of a written plan is its "erasability." Chances are it will be revised once or twice before it is submitted to the manager, and those revisions represent missteps not taken. How many of us wish we had more carefully considered our options before taking spontaneous action at work or, for that matter, in our personal lives? From a managerial perspective, written plans by subordinates offer deep insights into their critical-thinking skills.

The request for a written plan is, counterintuitively, all the more important during a crisis, when one might think there is no time for someone to sit at a desk and ponder possible courses of action. But an emergency is precisely the occasion to plan, because impulsive actions taken during an emergency are generally not recoverable. Given the fast pace of events, the attempt to correct that first misstep equates to two opportunities lost. Action plans don't have to be elaborate; they don't even have to be typed. A scribbled paragraph is better than nothing, because it sets the mind to thinking. The mere act of writing down one's intentions during an emergency exerts an illusory modicum of control over the situation. "Illusory" control at that point is okay because the confidence it creates soon manifests in the form of potent action and real control.

CHAPTER FOUR

Managing the Light at the End of the Tunnel

"Infiltrate" the customer all the way to the top • The FBI never gives up • Publish a Ten Most Wanted Customers list • Counter (and positively influence) unfair criticism

> I like the hunt.
>
> —SPECIAL AGENT (AND COLD CASE SPECIALIST) DON ROBERTS

Although the FBI is the subject of numerous action-packed movies and suspense novels, many of its real-life cases do not lend themselves well to dramatic reenactment. It would be like watching the grass grow. The infiltration of an organized crime family, for example, can take years. Domestic espionage cases during the cold war could require up to a decade of covert surveillance in order for the FBI to fully understand and exploit the needs and wants of a foreign spy. And some cold cases, "unsolved" crimes the Bureau never lets go of, have taken twenty years or more to finally crack.

The progress of such long-term investigation cannot always be demonstrated with the flourish attending a foiled bank heist or a happily resolved kidnapping case, and sometimes it cannot be demonstrated at all for fear of compromising the investigation. Management must evaluate these long-running cases with different metrics.

"It depends on who you're going up against and what you're trying to accomplish," explains Matt Heron. "The ultimate success metrics are indictments and convictions, but in the interim, we look for things like, (a) the number of sources an agent can develop, (b) the quality of their information, (c) the number of leads, (d) the number of undercover operations resulting from those leads, and (e) the number of crimes we think are prevented in the meantime."

How the FBI manages the light at the end of the tunnel may prove helpful to every CEO and manager who must sustain a long-term campaign to win over or regain a particularly prestigious customer or market segment.

"Infiltrate" the Customer All the Way to the Top

When the FBI goes after a vast criminal enterprise, its strategy is, in some ways, similar to the organization targeted. The Mob, for example, is always characterized in the press as having "tentacles" everywhere; the FBI conducts an equally multipronged investigation. The Mob "infiltrates" virtually all levels of society; the FBI likewise infiltrates all levels of the Mob. The Mob makes use of respectable front organizations; the fictitious enterprises created by the FBI's undercover strategists are equally convincing. The Mob is wary and operates in secrecy; the FBI wrote the book on clandestine operations.

If there is a fundamental difference it is this: The Mob is satisfied with less, whereas the FBI wants all the marbles. The organized crime families, that is, are realists. They know that Rome wasn't built in a day, and they are satisfied with manifold little victories here and there in drug trafficking, prostitution, cyber crime, gambling, the black market, etc. The FBI agents pursuing them, however, are idealists. They see no reason why a monstrous criminal enterprise cannot be completely conquered.

Assistant Director Stephen Tidwell puts it this way: "We detect, disrupt, and dismantle the criminal enterprise until there is not a brick left standing."

When an organization like the FBI comes out of the box with the stated goal of unconditional victory, it strikes a certain tenor in the "marketplace" of organized crime. No organized crime leader wants FBI agents on his tail because he knows that a relentless process is about to unfold. He knows, too, that there are no little sacrifices he can make that will satiate the beast. The FBI is not content with arresting the soldiers. It is after the general.

"Ideally, when you work a drug case or a Mob case," explains retired undercover agent and FBI legend Jack García, "you want to take the head of the organization. You want to keep going up and up and up within the structure until you can't go any higher, and then dismantle the entire organization from top to bottom."

The FBI's penchant for going all the way to the top is indicative of a definition of success that may elude the public some of the time and elude the media all the time. It bespeaks patience and determination and a certain obliviousness to demands for immediate results. A long-term investigation that ultimately destroys a criminal enterprise would have ample opportunities for showcase arrests—replete with displays for the evening news programs of confiscated drugs, weapons, and currency—if the FBI wanted to satisfy the general public's longing for visible results. But those little victories would have pulled the rug out from under the true thrust of the investigation and alerted the kingpins at the top of the organization to the danger of which they were theretofore unaware.

It also demonstrates how willingly the FBI will postpone its own gratification. An investigation into a nefarious criminal organization requires restraint and discipline on the part of every agent involved. The rules of procedure act as a kind of governor on the zealous agent, but the goal of unconditional victory is a constant reminder not to let one's righteous indignation get in the way. FBI agents who see firsthand the damage caused by the drug cartels must occasionally be tempted to end the investigation immediately and slap handcuffs on as many dealers, punks, and pimps as possible just to get them off the street *now*. But when the agents recall that the human suffering they witness in their own domain is simultaneously taking place in dozens of cities, and that it may all be directly attributable to one cartel figure at the top, the long-term perspective is regained.

And when the day of reckoning finally comes for the crime bosses, who seemed so invulnerable for so many years, neither they nor the public can quite believe it. The expressions on the faces of handcuffed, high-level Mafia "executives," brought out into the light of day by implacable agents, often show an inability to accept that this is really happening. Accustomed to flattering obeisance at restaurants, nightclubs, and in all of their dealings, they look more confused than indignant as they are led against their will through a gauntlet of press reporters and into the waiting police vans. The sense of accomplishment experienced by the agents responsible for such high-level arrests transcends the boundaries of their own particular stomping grounds, because the indictments and convictions that follow could well be of national and even international consequence. By getting the "general" they have routed an entire army of foot soldiers.

This "going to the top" mind-set of the FBI would serve us well in our own business strategies. Clearly we do business with companies, sometimes significant business, without ever having "targeted" their CEO. Often we haven't even met the CEO. And when a major order comes in, we tend to focus on what we have in hand rather than on all else that is available from that particular customer, most of which is being awarded to our competitors.

Why are we satisfied with so little?

There are several factors that make us settle for less. For one, we are under a great deal of pressure to perform, to meet demands and expectations from the shareholder, through the board of directors, and down the chain of command. These demands are transmitted in the form of goals, assigned at each level. These goals inherit new margins each time they are passed on, burdening the hapless field representative with the built-in margins of several managers.

The boss's rhetorical question, "What have you done for me lately?" is best answered in the short term by holding up a new order from the customer. The "going to the top" strategy of the FBI requires such a long-term view of one's relationship to the company and to the customer that it is difficult to implement. Those who are held on a short leash and evaluated on a quarterly basis—salespeople, sales managers, and sometimes even CEOs—

will gratefully take what they can now rather than plan a long-term strategy. This is not to suggest that an immediate order from the customer is contrary to our long-term wishes; quite the reverse: Every order is a beachhead for further progress with the customer. But when the pressure to perform is intense, we are likely to spend our energy taking the easiest path to more orders, and that means continuing to deal with our established customer contacts rather than risk the contact's displeasure by going around established protocol all the way to the top.

But the hard truth is that if our customer contact is not a gateway, she is an obstacle. And many key customer contacts, who relish their positions of power, are not gateways. In fact, the Very Important Buyer, whom salespeople wine and dine, may be quite possessive of her authority. If so, her answers as to the identity of the decision makers above her will be vague and her introductions to associates rare. *She* wants to be the point of contact and jealously guards that position. Ironically, the salesperson may feel equally proprietary and not want to introduce his own associates into the account. He also wants to be the company liaison on all matters relating to his key customer. Management cannot tolerate either situation because a single relationship is too fragile a bridge. Anything can happen. The buyer may retire or otherwise leave her company; she may change loyalties; she may come to expect rewards for the business she gives; she may not be "in the loop" in her own organization in terms of future sales and service opportunities; and, at the very least, she may keep her other suppliers (your competitors!) on their toes by awarding them business as well. The salesperson, of course, is also a free agent who may leave the company with two weeks' notice, hardly enough time to build a new bridge. Worse yet, he may take the key customer with him.

The suggestion that the supplier of goods or services should develop a strategy to "infiltrate" its major customers all the way to the top of the organization may seem a bit insidious, but that is precisely what every supplier should do if it wants to serve its customer optimally in the long term. It is also, incidentally, what the customer is doing or should be doing with its own customers. Establishing relationships at every level of the customer's hierarchy, including the senior executive and CEO level, is not only in the self-interest of the supplier, it is equally important to the customer. The stronger the supplier, the better position he will be in to serve, especially in times of material shortages and economic downturns. And the more the supplier knows of the long-term aspirations of his customer, the better he can join hands and walk that path with the customer. This information is rarely gathered from one point of contact. The pieces of the puzzle are taken from many points of view, then assembled at a thoughtful strategy meeting, which will determine the best way to serve the customer not only today but well into the future.

And it is this long-term view that will sustain a team approach to "infiltrate" the customer. If the salesperson's key contact is possessive of her position of authority, the salesperson should not try to make an end run around her, but management must—by sending emissaries from other departments. Representatives from customer service, IT, accounts receivable, manufacturing, quality control, and senior management all have legitimate reasons for establishing relationships with their counterparts at a major customer; the more they know about the customer the better they can serve. There is absolutely nothing wrong with wanting to get to know our customer better and for wanting our customer to become better acquainted with our own operations, our own aspirations.

Although it is preferable with a team approach to establish counterpart relationships on the executive level, the foot soldier should not be afraid to introduce himself or herself to the CEO of an important customer. But what gives many sales and customer service representatives pause is the apparent insularity of that chief exec. Protected by concentric circles of executive secretaries and assistants, who close ranks at every intrusion, the CEO's office seems impenetrable. Moreover, we are intimidated by the unquestioned protocol of generations. It seems to us audacious, almost in bad taste, to try to bypass the normal chain of command, established not only to run the organization but to protect the CEO. So entrenched is our respect for protocol that we fear the backlash of having violated it. Wouldn't the "targeted" CEO be affronted at our offered handshake? Wouldn't he or she be concerned at the breach of corporate etiquette and wonder how we managed to slip through the very people hired to deal with underlings like us?

There is also the concern that even if we did somehow get through to the CEO, he or she might not be interested in talking to us. What would a general have in common with a foot soldier? But to think this way is to underestimate the natural insecurities of the CEO. Despite the air of authority, despite the calm and assured demeanor, the CEO has his or her share of worries, wakes up in the middle of the night occasionally at some nightmare business scenario, and is therefore always pleased to find allies on the battlefield of the marketplace. Key suppliers are very important to the CEO. As a supplier's rep, you are on the CEO's team too. By "getting to the top" you have shown both resourcefulness and courage—attributes that will serve the CEO's company as well as yours.

Of course, it must be borne in mind that CEOs can be fired or otherwise forced or tempted to leave our customer's organization. Our business relationship with any one individual, no matter how powerful, will always be at risk. The definition of "the top" must be expanded to include significant investors who hold influential power, various members of the board of directors, and members of the executive steering committee. The deeper the customer can be "infiltrated," the more likely an enduring, profitable relationship can be developed.

The FBI does not necessarily focus all its efforts against the formal structure of the targeted enterprise. It may infiltrate from oblique angles, by developing points of contact on the periphery (for instance, the friend of a friend who will one day unknowingly facilitate an introduction). Our customers may also be approached from oblique angles, by finding common cause outside the walls of the actual business. The CEO or a member of the executive team may be very active in a particular charity, community development project, or not-for-profit social service. Generally speaking, people interested in similar public service endeavors share many core values. It is not at all cynical to consider establishing rapport with a customer through common-cause activities that have nothing to with business but everything to do with a better community or world. The approach is oblique but not necessarily deceptive. Many people have joined Rotary, Optimist, or Lions clubs initially for the business contacts they hoped to make, only to find after a few years that service to the community is such a liberating experience that the incidental benefits to one's own business scarcely come to mind.

The FBI's infiltration "all the way to the top" is all the more impressive when one considers that its investigations are often begun without knowing the identity of the "chief executive" of the criminal organization; indeed the investigation may be launched to discover his identity. If the FBI can get to the head of a global criminal enterprise, when the identity of that kingpin may be initially unknown and jealously guarded throughout the mission by his deadly minions, certainly we in private enterprise can establish personal contact with our customer's CEO.

As a footnote to this discussion, the same vertical strategy should be applied internally, within one's own organization. Why is it so many otherwise gregarious employees suddenly turn into chameleons when their CEO walks by? Possibly they simply want to appear busy and focused on their tasks. But it is also possible they fear being asked questions by the CEO that might be difficult to answer credibly. Or, to give them the benefit of the doubt, employees may not want to interrupt the CEO in his or her train of thought. Certainly, few employees will take the initiative to walk up, stick out their hand, and introduce themselves for fear it might be regarded as apple polishing by their associates.

Here again, we may be underestimating the CEO's need for a show of support. We have been told time and again by the popular business culture that it is "lonely at the top." If that is so, doesn't it follow that the CEO would be delighted to meet a kindred soul? If courage is a valued attribute, would the CEO be pleased to see it manifested by one of his or her own employees? By making it a habit to go "all the way to the top of the organization," the employee just may end up there on a permanent basis.

The FBI Never Gives Up

Special Agent Don Roberts is right out of central casting for the part of an FBI agent. Tall, very fit, and tough as nails, he entered the room being used for interviews with the look of a man who could think of better things to do than talk to a writer. I introduced myself and received a bone-crushing handshake. Sitting down, I fiddled with the tape recorder, waiting for the blood to flow back into my fingers. He took a seat and stared at me. His eyes gave the impression he could read minds—and that he didn't like what was in mine. Under his gaze, I suddenly wanted to confess to every overdue library book fine I had never paid.

Don is a manhunter. He is known throughout the agency as one of the best when it comes to tracking down fugitives who have fled the country to evade arrest. In fact, he had just wrapped up a fugitive case by catching the suspect wanted in connection with the murder of a thirteen-year-old girl.

Ten years after the crime!

In 1996, Sophia Briseño was brutally murdered in the otherwise peaceful little town of Murrieta, California, not far from Don's field office in Riverside. Don had read about the murder in the newspaper. With a daughter of his own that age, he offered his assistance to the Murrieta Police Department detectives who had jurisdiction. The local detectives, however, were on top of the case and soon identified eighteen-year-old Crispin Solorio García of Mexico as their prime suspect. After their investigation, García was charged with murder by the Riverside County district attorney's office. But by then, García had fled the state.

The Murrieta detectives, who did not have the resources to pursue García to the ends of the earth, came to the FBI for help. Don obtained a federal arrest warrant for unlawful flight to avoid prosecution and was officially on the case, almost exactly one year after the crime had been committed.

"I had the casebook on my desk from that time," explains the veteran agent. "In it were some family photos and also, of course, the graphic and heartbreaking crime scene photos. Not a day went by when I didn't think of that little girl."

Agent Roberts, however, never thought of the crime as a cold case. "I don't really think of any case as cold or hot. This guy was wanted for murder. It didn't matter whether he did it yesterday or ten years ago; he took a life. A family was grieving."

But after a year the case had "cooled" to some degree in terms of leads to the whereabouts of the suspect. "He was an illegal immigrant, without identification, without any kind of documentation, such as a Social Security number, during his stay here. All we had was a driver's license photo and a right thumbprint. We weren't even sure of his real name or of his family's whereabouts. All we knew was that the Murrieta detectives were pretty sure he had crossed the border. And Mexico is a big country, without any kind of centralized database that could help in a hunt for a fugitive."

Don had other casebooks on his desk too, with clues that had to be followed while they were "hot," lest these cases too turned "cold." Other grieving families were counting on him to find their assailants. Juggling all the cases to the best of his ability, he cherished every tidbit of information he could gather on the Sophia Briseño investigation.

"As long as I moved the case forward in some way, I felt better about it. If I identified the phone number of a relative or found one of his childhood friends, I felt I was making progress because this information might lead to another tidbit of information. And I would think, 'Maybe tomorrow the big break will come.' You don't know where the finish line is until you're there."

Often, when seeking information, Don had to play his

highest card—the crime scene photos. "Friends and family members are usually in denial. They don't believe the person they know could be guilty of anything, much less a brutal murder. But when they see the graphic photos, sometimes something shakes loose. You would have to have a heart of stone not to be affected."

But each new lead took months of painstaking, incredibly detailed work. And with each new month came a kind of remorse. "When I say I thought about the Sophia Briseño case every day, it came with a fair amount of guilt for not yet having found the person. I didn't find him a year after I started. I didn't find him five years after I started. I didn't find him eight years after I started. And meanwhile I'm spending so much time on other cases that in some ways are easier because the clues are fresh. But there are only so many hours in a day. I have a family. And I have to sleep sometime. Nonetheless I felt guilt."

In the tenth year of the investigation, Don's relentless patience paid off. He was fairly confident he had traced García to a small town in Michoacán, Mexico. The Mexican authorities were contacted. If there had been any lack of interest on their part, it vanished at the sight of the crime scene photos. "They have daughters, too," observes Don.

García was positively identified. On June 1, 2007—ten years after the crime—a provisional arrest warrant for the extradition of Mr. García was executed. Upon completion of his jail sentence for unrelated charges, García will be transported to Mexico City to await extradition. In all likelihood, the man who will come to pick him up will be Agent Don Roberts.

"When I heard he had been identified," recalls Don, "I was elated. I couldn't wait to tell the Briseño family and the Murrieta detectives who had solved the case." In fact,

Don and the lead detective, still with the Murrieta Police Department, went together to break the good news. "It was very moving. The mother sat down and cried. Then she hugged us. It was good that we got him, but the sad fact was Sophia would have been twenty-three years old had her life not been taken."

"Cold Cases" in Private Enterprise

The business equivalent of the cold case is, of course, the lost customer. And while there are examples of "Amazing Grace" in the marketplace—when a customer "once was lost but now is found"—the prospect of renewed business with a customer who has long ago forsaken us can seem very unlikely indeed. The reasons for this are many: (a) the lost customer has taken up with another supplier who treats him like a king and gives him no cause to entertain another bid; (b) the current generation of salespeople regard the lost customer as not worth the investment of time and effort when there are many other "hot" leads to pursue; (c) there is a market share mentality in many sales departments that accepts the divvying up of customers as right and proper; (d) the salespeople console themselves with the fact that their competition has lost customers too, happily serviced by their own company; (e) the salespeople fear that the "original sin" of poor service on the part of the company has not been forgotten. The long and short of it is that "cold business" tends to remain cold for many, many years.

The practicality of pursuing a lost customer is also daunting. Who are you going to ask to go after him? Most salespeople are rewarded with commissions or bonuses for *new* business and would strongly resent being saddled with an assignment where the odds were a million to one against success. Even if they accepted the "mission impossible" with good grace, it would only be lip service; little quality time would be spent pursuing a customer who cannot be caught. It simply wouldn't pencil out. In fact, even the sales manager who assigned the lost cause—and who is evaluated on a quarterly basis for the sales revenue his or her team brings in—would not long tolerate the energy being spent on a sales activity that might not come to fruition until long after he or she has left the company.

Few publicly owned companies have the courage and the stamina required to sustain a campaign that does not show immediate promise. The board of directors, under pressure from the shareholders, wants results now. Commitments made to Wall Street must be met. How could a CEO possibly justify the use of precious corporate resources on what impatient investors would regard as a pipe dream? Can we imagine the visionary leader of a corporation standing before an annual gathering of shareholders with charts and graphs chronicling a fruitless venture? Such a CEO would seem eccentric, obsessed with the past. The shareholders would demand a leader who lived in the real world and who pursued realistic goals—not a Captain Ahab.

But there are reasons why even an irrevocably lost customer can be a realistic goal in a dynamic marketplace. There may have been a change of leadership, which suggests that our sins may be forgotten, if not forgiven. Or our competitor may stumble and have supply problems of its own. The lost customer may branch out into a new product line or into uncharted territory where we may be better positioned to be of service. And perhaps we too have changed! Our customer service has dramatically improved, as has our quality control. The human body is said to completely renew itself on a cellular level every seven years, and so has our company been renewed. What is needed is someone like agent Don Roberts to patiently court the lost customer and to monitor the incremental or dynamic changes taking place with that organization.

If not handled properly, it would be a managerial challenge to make the lost customer assignment seem attractive to the best salesperson in the organization, for the job of bringing the wayward customer back into the fold *would* require your best talent. Being a top performer, she will already be inordinately busy bringing much-needed revenue into the company coffers and meeting performance metrics you have set for her. She will resent being tasked with a long-term, time-consuming sales activity that does not promise to benefit her anytime soon, and the sales manager will hate to ask her to do it, because the manager's own job depends upon her short-term performance.

But FBI agents are busy too. And they too have performance metrics expected of them, which are more readily met by working on cases in the here and now. It's conceivable that even the most dedicated agent might resent being handed a case that the best minds have not been able to solve for decades—at a time when his or her current caseload already requires fourteen-hour days. There is also one's career to think of. Surely the gratification that comes from racking up a lot of indictments makes those long days and nights worthwhile. One can no doubt rack up many successes in the time it takes to investigate one solitary cold case that no one has yet been able to crack.

Special Agent Mary Hogan, another of the Bureau's best cold case specialists, is the first to admit to mixed emotions whenever she is handed an investigation with a long history. "There is an intimidation factor. I mean, you ask yourself, 'If these agents before me—all of them diligent—couldn't solve the case after ten years, how am I going to do it?'"

Mary, at a petite five feet two, seems the very opposite of hard-boiled manhunter Don Roberts, yet she is equally relentless. Two of her most recently concluded cases were positively ancient by most standards. Derrick Stevens, a bank robber who had evaded law enforcement for seventeen years (and had taken on a new identity as a senior manager at a university), finally grew so distracted by the haunting presence of Mary Hogan, always one step behind him, that he gave himself up. As a kind of tribute to her persistence, he insisted on surrendering to Mary in person on the steps of the Los Angeles field office. Mary was also instrumental in the arrest of "soccer mom" Kathleen Soliah—formerly domestic terrorist Sarah Jane Olson, who had been evading law enforcement and living under her assumed name for twenty-five years!

Like Don Roberts, Mary personalizes each case. She's currently working on an unsolved bombing-murder from 1985, yet as far as she's concerned, it might have happened yesterday. "The victim is always on my mind. I've met his family and sat in their living room with his pictures all around. I carry a photo of him, taken when he was alive." Blinking back sudden tears, she adds, "And he's still alive in me."

Personalizing the lost customer, perhaps by keeping a scrapbook of current articles on his or her company, may also help the salesperson keep the goal "alive" and fresh in the mind. If a goal is ever-present, it is deemed by the subconscious as achievable. If the former customer is regarded as a memory and not as a living, breathing CEO who is giving his or her business to somebody else, the long-lost customer will forever be associated with the company's past, not its future.

Assistant Director Stephen Tidwell suggests, with a smile, that a cold case is an opportunity to "prove you are smarter than anyone else." He is alluding to the disproportionate sense of triumph and satisfaction that comes with solving an "unsolvable" case. Surely the Bureau sits up and takes note of such an achievement. It's got to be a feather in the cap of the agent responsible, and a big feather at that.

But solving a cold case has additional merit. When Don Roberts finally tracked down the elusive killer of that innocent girl, ten years after the fact, he demonstrated something about the FBI—and about himself—that deters the rational criminal mind from certain acts. As impressive as it is to capture a bank robber twenty minutes after the robbery, the criminal community doubtless ascribes a certain amount of bad luck to that bank robber. Perhaps, it might reason, if the operation had been better planned, or if the bank robber had not been spotted by a citizen with a cell phone, he might have gotten away with it. But how does the criminal reconcile to himself the FBI's relentless pursuit of a killer across time and space? It has to be frightening. It's more fundamental than "the long arm of the law" in action. It must seem to the criminal like the haunting embodiment of conscience itself, implacable and inescapable.

Don Roberts sees no moral distinction between a cold case and a recent crime, which means he accepts the additional workload of a cold case with equanimity. A salesperson who does not see any difference between a lost customer and a hot prospect, on the grounds that both represent "new" business to the company, would be a gift from heaven indeed.

To expect an employee in private enterprise to have the kind of proprietary devotion of Don Roberts and Mary Hogan is unreasonable, unless perhaps it is a family-owned company. But there are managerial steps that can be taken to cultivate at least a semblance of that kind of dedication. And the Tidwell approach is certainly a good start. Telling a salesperson that he or she has the opportunity to accomplish the unaccomplished by "capturing" a lost customer is perfectly true as far as it goes. That it would be quite an achievement is also true. But unlike the FBI agent, the salesperson is wondering, "What's in it for me?" and that question must be answered.

Certainly a higher commission rate for new business from lost customers would be in order, followed by the assurance of management that the salesperson responsible would "own" that account for as long as he or she stayed with the company. Since such an achievement bespeaks managerial potential, the intrepid salesperson should be cultivated to think in terms of a career with the organization. That sense of ownership would help foster the long-term view required for much unrewarded time and energy. Stock options would add to the perception of ownership. Management might also offer a liberal expense account, since the salesperson would be expected to join the organizations, and perhaps the country club, that would place the salesperson in proximity to the lost customer.

Setting performance metrics and monitoring the progress of a lost customer campaign would call for a delicate balance of push and protect. The salesperson, who has a built-in excuse for nonperformance—a customer with a notorious history of antagonism toward the company—must be prodded to take the initiative. And just as Don Roberts took pleasure in the tiniest bit of meaningful progress in the investigation, the salesperson would have to be applauded for noting subtle changes in the organization of the lost customer. He or she would also at times have to be protected from falling into despair at the lack of apparent progress. Salespeople thrive on recognition, and it would be management's responsibility to heap praise on the salesperson for his or her tenacity.

It is interesting to note that agent Don Roberts considers himself lucky to be able to pursue cold cases under the FBI's new counterterrorism paradigm. "Finding the killer of a thirteen-year-old girl," he admits, "is somewhat down the list of our new, post 9/11 priorities. But I feel blessed that I've been allowed to continue this work. We're all doing things that we feel are very important."

Similarly, the corporate "agent" who pursues lost business must feel the importance of his or her work to the well-being of the company and all of its employees; to his or her own career; and to the lost customer as well, who will presumably benefit greatly by coming back into the fold.

Publish a Ten Most Wanted Customers List

In the elevator lobby of the Los Angeles Federal Building, where everybody can see it, the FBI's Ten Most Wanted list is posted conspicuously on the wall. People who work for other agencies housed in the building may walk by without a glance at the posters. But when an FBI agent or one of the Bureau's support personnel passes by, he or she casts a sharp eye at the display, as if the photographs were bull's-eyes.

FBI agents do not, over the years, develop a blasé attitude toward the Ten Most Wanted poster display they see every morning on their way into the office and every evening as they leave. They can tell you the particulars of each poster pinned to the bulletin board, the height and weight of the fugitive, the aliases used, the crimes committed, the sparse biographical re-marks, and the reward offered ($25 million in the case of Osama bin Laden). While the average citizen may look at the posters from the hopeless perspective of his or her own limited sphere of acquaintances, the agent is much more optimistic, conscious of a nationwide and global network of law enforcement profes-sionals who will scour the earth until these fugitives are caught. They can't wait for the day when a banner with the word "cap-tured" is added to a poster.

"There's nothing that will get an office more excited than hearing it has a 'top tenner' in its territory," says Assistant Di-rector Stephen Tidwell, with a smile a "top tenner" never wants to see.

The FBI's Ten Most Wanted list would be a powerful moti-vator if it were strictly an internal communiqué within the Bu-reau. But when it is broadcast to the world at large, its effect surely is multiplied. By making the list public, the FBI is lever-aging its force of ten thousand agents by the general population, but it also has created a whole new level of "oversight." Now the public knows if the FBI is "doing its job." While public pres-sure to perform is not necessary for an FBI agent to go the extra mile, it must have been wonderful to finally still the cries of "Where is Patty Hearst?"

Companies would do well to consider having their own equivalent of a Ten Most Wanted Customers list, and for reasons similar to those of the FBI.

A top ten list of "most wanted" customers, if posted con-spicuously, would alert all within the organization—from the boardroom to the mail room—of the desired business that is still "roaming free." Why shouldn't that be common knowledge? It might surprise many a CEO to discover how few employees in the wide organization have even an inkling of the top targets of the sales department.

The effect could be galvanizing. The list would be a constant reminder of the most desirable accounts "out there" in the marketplace. Each "poster" would be modeled after the real thing, with a flattering photo of the CEO the company wants to do business with, some organizational stats, and perhaps a "reward" to the employee who contributes to the establishment of business relations. Every employee would be "in the know" and explicitly recruited in the quest. And one never knows what can happen when the entire workforce is being leveraged. For example, a clerk in accounts payable may have a friend who works in the "top tenner" company's purchasing department. A delivery man may have noticed something unusual while driving by the company, such as a strange truck pulling away from the loading dock, suggesting a change of vendors. An IT tech may have read something on an industry blog that portends change (and opportunity!) within the top tenner's infrastructure. These little bits and pieces of information could be helpful to the company's strategists. But the information will not be communicated unless the rank and file is involved in the hunt for new business. A conspicuous top ten list would keep the company's goals fresh in everyone's mind, especially if there were to be a reward (such as a tropical vacation for two) for information leading to the "capture" of the client.

By publishing its list of top ten target customers (for example, through conspicuous ads and commercials), the company would, like the FBI, invite the pressure of the public. Stockholders would ask about the progress of reining in the top ten accounts at every shareholder meeting. Business journalists would reference the list and perhaps even make fun of its ambitiousness. The current suppliers of the top ten companies would be put on notice that determined competition is coming after them and is not afraid to say so. And the targeted customers? They would love it!

Just imagine a CEO picking up the *Wall Street Journal* and seeing his own "wanted" photo posted and his company listed as the stated business goal of a vendor—publicly, fearlessly, audaciously. The impression could be nothing but positive. The name of the vendor would be forever ingrained in the CEO's consciousness. He would investigate. What kind of company is it? And look! One of the top ten has been "captured" and is now doing business with this audacious supplier. The CEO might call that company and ask about its experience with the bold supplier, or he might tell his purchasing department to entertain a quote. He might say to himself, "Surely a vendor willing to go to these lengths—publicly—to acquire my business would do much in the way of customer service to keep it."

To carry this somewhat fanciful, but eminently doable metaphor further, there would even be a certain amount of public pressure exerted on the target customer. He might be asked by his own shareholders or board of directors, "Why haven't you done business with this vendor who has laid their reputation on the line to work with you? Have you at least spoken to them?"

A vendor is known by its customers. That's why so many marketing campaigns are eager to list the prestigious organizations already being served. But a vendor can also be known by the customers it *wants* to serve. The higher the ambition, the stronger the company looks—for surely it wouldn't aspire to serve a premier customer if it couldn't actually provide the service. A supplier with the courage to take on such an imaginative initiative as a Ten Most Wanted Customers list would surely be a salient feature on the business landscape. When supplier and customer are equally prominent for their visionary leadership, there is every reason to establish and maintain a business relationship.

The interesting thing about the FBI's Ten Most Wanted list is that it does not diminish with success—there is a replacement for every captured suspect. It's always a top ten list. The same should be true with the commercial equivalent. For every customer captured, another must take its place. Thus, the vendor's work is never done. It continues to strive in a most public way. Year after year the target companies will change, to the gratification of the vendor's employees and other stakeholders—and, of course, to the gratification of the well-served customer. The market as a whole will take note. A company with the courage to post and maintain a top ten list of desired customers will distinguish itself from all the organizations without the courage to do likewise.

Counter (and Positively Influence) Unfair Criticism

The sensitive nature of the FBI's covert "war on terror" makes the Bureau particularly vulnerable to outside criticism for a number of reasons. The progress of these long-term investigations often cannot be reported for fear of jeopardizing related operations. "Progress," in fact, may require months or years of patient commitment to materialize. Antiterror operations are complicated, global in scope, and difficult to reduce to a story line. And it is often difficult if not impossible for the FBI to correct the public record should the Bureau be mischaracterized, especially regarding investigations where the safety and the efficacy of courageous undercover agents might be compromised.

"It's a little different if we bust twenty-five gangbangers," explains Special Agent in Charge (SAC) Robert Loosle, "because then we can hold a press conference and stand tall next to the display of weapons we've harvested. But there are agents here and in the CIA who are doing incredible jobs that no one will ever hear about. On top of that, their agency is getting bashed."

Although the FBI wouldn't put it in quite these terms, the Bureau feels entitled to a little slack from the news media when it comes to coverage of highly sensitive covert operations that cannot be commented upon in all but the most general terms.

So it was only natural that when Assistant Director John Miller slammed down the February 7, 2008, issue of *Rolling Stone* magazine—which featured a long article likening the FBI to a "Fear Factory" that cranked out investigations based on "concocted threats" in order to prop up its own role in a hyperbolized war on terror— steam came out of his ears.

A former journalist himself who once served as chief of counterterrorism for the Los Angeles Police Department, Miller was not only irked by the mischaracterization but by what he considered a lack of professionalism. Seated at his computer, he pounded out a response to the editors of *Rolling Stone*. "Before coming to the FBI," he began, "I won most of the major awards that they give to a reporter. I feel I have standing to say that a journalist has an obligation to tell at least two sides of a story. Your readers only got one." Miller then proceeded to take the article apart point by point, strongly disputing the charge that his agency pursued trumped-up investigations.

"In almost every case heard by a jury," he wrote, "the defendants were found guilty, in spite of having some dedicated and talented defense lawyers articulate the same claims Mr. Lawson has swallowed. The Yassin Aref case in Albany, New York, and the Hamid Hayat case in Lodi, California, are two examples. In other cases such as the 'Lackawanna Six,' and the Torrance cell, the defendants pled guilty with the advice of counsel."

To its credit, *Rolling Stone* published Miller's letter (followed by a point-by-point response from the author of the article). The FBI "published" Miller's letter as well, in the form of a blistering press release that can be found online at the FBI's website.

It may have come as something of a surprise to the magazine editors that the FBI was willing to so vociferously take them on. After all, we don't normally expect "public servants" to hit back. But the FBI does not turn the other cheek after the publication or broadcast of a particularly critical news story when it deems the criticism to be unfair. Within hours of a report that strikes the agency as grossly unfair, strong press releases from FBI headquarters or the local field office are issued to correct the public record. FBI execs are not shy about contacting the newspaper, magazine, or television station responsible and asking for an opportunity to rebut.

It's not because the Bureau is thin-skinned. It's because it has people working for it who are, collectively, a national treasure and who deserve the moral support of the organization.

"Sometimes I'll read an op-ed piece," explains Assistant Director Stephen Tidwell, "where somebody without any due diligence, and without the most fundamental investigation, will throw a rock at the FBI and at the agents who are working their hearts out to keep this country safe. In those cases, I'll pick it up and throw it right back. All I ask," he grins, "is that you get to know us better before you call us 'stupid.'"

Business—especially big business—can learn a lot from the FBI's spunky attitude toward the media, because it too is so often vilified in the press and on the evening news and in Hollywood portrayals. Many executives shy away from media interviews for fear of being ambushed with provocative and self-incriminating questions from a "crusading" journalist, or of being edited out of context later. And certainly no executive wants to make an enemy of an anchorman on the nightly news. The executive's reluctance to take on the media goes a little deeper—he or she doesn't want to alienate any portion of the company's customer base. The prevailing philosophy seems to be to hunker down until the storm passes or to send out a public relations spokesperson with a boilerplate response.

Corporate silence in the face of accusations from the media is interpreted by the general public as a tacit admission. "Why else are they not responding?" asks the public. An indignant rank and file, working under the pall of unjustified negative publicity, asks the same question. If the firm's leadership does not stand up for the firm, it is up to the manager to do so—quietly. Management must shelter its people from the storm. Employees bring their personal lives to work with them, and if they're down in the mouth because of undeserved criticism from the outside, then the workplace has to be made better than the "outside." The office or the factory must occasionally be a sanctuary as well as a locus of production.

High morale often has less to do with creature comforts and

perks and more to do with knowing that "we"—the rank and file, middle and senior management, and executive leadership— "are all in this together." Employee morale in the face of a hostile media is definitely a leadership issue and is too often ignored. No business leader wants his or her employees equivocating when someone asks them what they do for a living. Employees who do not feel good about what they are doing will cost the company in lost production, absenteeism, and turnover.

Press releases may not seem at first glance to have the emotional impact of a righteously indignant CEO grabbing the microphone in defense of the corporation. But press releases are usually more substantive. The facts are there in black and white, refuting the hurtful allegations point by point, and these facts give the rank and file ammunition with which to answer their friends and neighbors. Press releases are also more easily cited and more readily transmitted throughout the rank and file, which after all is the true target audience. Being written, press releases also have a tantalizingly legal aspect, as if there is a possibility they are being laid down as part of the framework of a broader action.

But the employees want to hear from their leaders as well. If the CEO is silent, the middle manager can revive the morale of his or her subordinates by simply telling the truth from the company's perspective and by answering all questions frankly. The source of the criticism and its track record for accuracy and honesty is also fair game. Criticism from a news station or from a publication that has been off the mark in the past or has been driven by an agenda can easily be blunted. But perhaps the most important case the manager can make is the moral case, because this is the area in which confusion most often reigns. The moral argument from one's critics is also the most difficult to counter.

There is, for example, a moral case to be made for energy independence (national security, the freedom to travel, economic independence) or for drug research (combating the great medical challenges of our time) or for building skyscraper condominiums (so that people can live close to their work and reduce freeway congestion). And, yes, there is even a moral argument for increased profits. Profits make continued research and development possible; profits increase the value of the company stock (owned by increasing numbers of employees); profits create more jobs for more Americans; profits mean job security.

But what about the industries for which that argument is difficult to make? It may be impossible for the manager to make a moral case for alcohol and tobacco products, except in terms of an individual's right to purchase them in a free society. But even in these industries, the manager must not be shy. These products, after all, are legal and desired by adults for the pleasures they give. The purchase of these products benefits society through health and education programs supported by consumer-paid taxes. If these products were not manufactured responsibly, a black market would appear selling substitutions of dubious quality, like the bathtub gin that ruined so many lives during Prohibition.

Whatever the message and whichever the industry, it must be sincere, from the lips of unapologetic managers who confidently confront the negative characterizations of the company and of the industry. The manager can begin by making sure every employee has a clear idea of the value of his or her product or service. That means the employee must be educated, not with buzzwords and not through brainwashing, but by an honest presentation of the facts. Many execs would be appalled at how little the average employee knows about the company's product or service. The rank and file must be shown in what ways its product is superior to the competition's and in what ways it contributes to the general welfare of human beings on a local, national, and even global level. So instead of the usual corporate pep talks, which are often thinly veiled exhortations to produce more goods and services, classroom-type discussion groups could be set up to both educate and motivate. This would be a wonderful opportunity for managers, in a teaching role, to field frank questions from the rank and file and to dispel the popular myths being bandied about the pop culture with reference to their specific industry and product. No doubt there will be employees who are sincerely conflicted about their work. And it is up to their leadership to make sure they arrive at work every morning with a smile on the face and a fire in the belly.

Educate Your Critics!

The FBI has found that not all mischaracterizations by the media are malicious. Sometimes news reporters or Hollywood directors are frankly ignorant of FBI procedures and simply decide to fill in the blanks themselves. By opening its doors to the media, the Bureau has increased the odds that accurate representations will be forthcoming.

"The Director has mandated," explains SAC Rob Grant, "that every FBI field office in the nation runs a Citizens Academy Program, which is a six-week class, once a year. Here in Chicago, we have thirty 'seats,' which are usually taken by civil rights organizations, community leadership groups, and people from the business community. But we reserve five seats for members of the press. These classes put the personal touch on who and what the FBI is. Almost without exception, the feedback we get is 'I had no idea how much work went into putting together a criminal investigation.' Or 'I didn't realize the constraints you folks work under.' It's really a great program."

A little education can go a long way toward more accurate reporting or more realistic screen portrayals, but the person-to-person contact is also productive. News reporters and film directors learn firsthand that FBI agents are not quite the cold, calculating observers once thought and that they have a sense of humor, share baby photos, and are eager to help. Relationships are formed and a certain level of trust is established. When a reporter is asked to "sit on a story" for forty-eight hours during a kidnapping case, there's a good chance he or she will comply. It's not that easy to refuse a favor requested in earnest by someone you have come to know. Similarly, when directing a scene depicting the FBI in action, a director may remember his or her contact at headquarters and consciously or subconsciously attempt an accurate portrayal so as not to disappoint.

There is a lesson to be learned here. The FBI's sunshine policy with the media illuminates an option for every manager plagued by internal criticism.

In an increasingly specialized and sometimes balkanized workplace, departments often vie against each other for limited corporate resources, just as individuals compete for the few-and-far-between promotions upline. It is a fact that sometimes our strongest adversary is not an outside competitor, but an associate. That we are all members of the corporate "family" is not particularly reassuring; arguments within a real family circle can be less restrained than those occurring outside. The higher we climb in management, the more likely our rivals will have the ear of senior leadership. So it's best to keep them on our side.

An individual, or an entire department, can be the subject of speculation and rumor simply because so little is known about the work being done behind closed doors. By facilitating a round-robin of open houses—department by department—for the benefit of management and all other interested parties, senior leadership could promote the kinds of cross-functional relationships that characterize high-performance organizations. At long last, we would learn why it takes accounting so long to process an expense report and how, on our own part, we can accelerate the process. We would discover why manufacturing really does need ninety days' lead time, how the service department manages to respond to customers all over the map, and how IT keeps the network up and running.

A program of regularly scheduled open house departmental tours, followed by frank question-and-answer sessions, could accomplish internally what the FBI's Citizens Academy Program accomplishes externally. A little education can go a long way toward promoting an unprecedented level of mutual trust and cooperation between formerly isolated departments. It is a simple enough concept, but one that would require the prodding of senior leadership and the enthusiastic support of middle management. The impact of such a policy could be disproportionate to the costs of the little downtime involved. An "open" organization dispels suspicion and encourages a level of communication between employees—formerly strangers—that can seem comparatively telepathic. Gossip, rumor, criticism, and antiquated concepts such as departmental "turf" do not take hold in an organization without walls.

There is every reason why an open-door policy should be extended to suppliers and to key customers. When one party is open and honest, the other feels compelled to reciprocate. When challenges are shared, mutually beneficial solutions are discussed. We may find that our key customers will step down from their pedestals and work with us peer to peer, while our suppliers step up to an equal footing and add to our strength. In any case, an open-door policy would intrigue our key customers and suppliers, and sooner or later they would accept the invitation.

CHAPTER FIVE

Managing Resources

Flying squads • Task-force management

> There are 800,000 law enforcement officers on the nation's
> streets every day. Compared to that, we've got roughly
> 10,000 FBI agents. Do the math. It makes sense to leverage.
>
> —JOE FORD, CHIEF OPERATING OFFICER, FBI

The public's conception of the FBI, propagated through news stories, television series, movies, suspense novels, and a bit of urban myth, is that of a dynamic organization with global reach, able to bring together vast resources from multiple points of origin to bear upon a crisis situation just about anywhere in the world. Whether the takedown of a terrorist cell is in Kansas City or Katmandu, we are confident the FBI can marshal the manpower, the technical assets, the logistical needs, and the firepower to take care of business. That may be in part because we associate the FBI with the U.S. government, which wields a budget in the trillions of dollars. We may never, unless prompted, think about the FBI in terms of an organization with limited finances (and virtually unlimited geographical responsibilities) that must allocate its money judiciously to departments clamoring for new or updated tools of the trade, find funding for long-term investigations, cut corners, tighten its belt, and arm wrestle its civilian suppliers for the best possible terms on national contracts (car leases, cell phones, air travel, out-of-town lodging, etc.)

The FBI cannot, like a business, deal with its needs by going out and making more money to pay for them. It must request its funding in competition with dozens of other agencies, each making its own pressing case. The FBI may have an advantage over some of the federal competition in that its responsibilities have to do with national security. But even in that realm it must compete with the Department of Homeland Security (DHS), CIA, National Security Agency (NSA), Secret Service, Bureau of Alcohol, Tobacco, and Firearms (ATF), Marshal's Service, U.S. Customs and Border Protection (CBP), Drug Enforcement Administration (DEA), Transportation Security Administration (TSA), etc., etc., plus the Army, Navy, Air Force, Marine Corps, and Coast Guard! And it must make its requests to a frequently unsympathetic, if not downright antagonistic, Congress. The FBI, in other words, is not all that different from the average corporation when it comes to having to count its pennies, and in some ways it is worse off.

Its resource-management solutions, therefore, will be of interest to us.

Flying Squads

In the aftermath of 9/11, Director Mueller stood before Congress and revealed the sweeping changes implemented to enable the FBI to better meet perhaps the greatest national security threat of the twenty-first century. Among the innovations suggested by Mueller was "the activation of flying squads to act as mobile resources in support of field operations."

John H. Pistole, executive assistant director of the FBI counterterrorism/counterintelligence section (and the legendary agent who once infiltrated the Mafia), explains: "We established flying squads—highly mobile response teams with specialized expertise in counterterrorism, languages, and analysis—to provide rapid, highly mobile support in terrorism investigations around the globe."

The FBI has had a global presence for many years. An FBI agent, referred to for decades in international parlance as a "legal attaché," holds down an office in each of the sixty U.S. embassies. In the event of a terrorist event, that agent may find himself or herself overwhelmed with all the duties and tasks involved in a major investigation. Not only is the legal attaché not staffed to cope with a really big case (terrorist bombing of a hotel, kidnapping of an American citizen or dignitary, etc.), he or she is under considerable pressure to report upline at all hours of the day to FBI headquarters, which may be several time zones away.

That legal attaché, stationed in a far-flung embassy, is not shy about picking up the phone, calling headquarters, and requesting a flying squad.

In the wee hours of the morning of August 5, 2003, such a call was received by Special Agent Michael Dehncke. Shaking himself awake, he listened to the sparse details known at that time of a suicide car bombing in the front lobby entrance of the JW Marriott Hotel in Setiabudi, South Jakarta, Indonesia. The blast killed 12 outright and injured 150. The voice on the other end of the phone told agent Dehncke his tickets on the next plane to Jakarta were ready.

Dehncke, like most flying squad members, is a bachelor, and it didn't take long for him to pack his bags. On his way to the airport, he listened to the world news reports, but he knew from previous experience that the bare facts of a news story tell so little. "Twelve killed" meant twelve human beings wantonly murdered as they innocently went about their business. "One hundred fifty injured" minimized the graphic truth. The term "injured" gives the impression that after suitable care, the casualties will soon be up and about, leading normal lives. It would have been much more appropriate to report "150 maimed, blinded, disfigured, and otherwise wounded for life," because that's what a car bomb packed with nuts and bolts and nails (often soaked in rat poison) does to flesh.

Even the announcement that the hotel would be closed for a few weeks seemed inadequate, because it gave a sense that things would pretty much return to normal after five weeks. But Dehncke had a clearer idea of why the terrorists attack economic targets. The rash of cancellations that immediately follows a hotel bombing is rarely referred to in the news, nor is the loss of future business for months or even years to come, nor crippling litigation costs, nor the overall damage to the national economy due to the subsequent and long-lasting drop in tourism nationwide.

The terrorists, he knew, were aware of the ripple effect of a hotel bombing even if the news media was not. They were, in this case, attacking Indonesia's economy by way of a soft target. The cost-damage ratio was disproportionately and grotesquely economical: one Toyota minivan, explosives, and a driver, compared to a billion rupees' worth of damage.

Agent Dehncke arrived in Jakarta none the worse for

wear after the long flight. His activities in the investigation are necessarily confidential, but suffice it to say that to date more than a dozen suspects have been convicted in connection with this bombing, their testimony confirming yet another cooperative terrorist operation between the Asian terror group Jemaah Islamiyah and Al-Qaeda.

Director Mueller's flying squad initiative has been put to good use in investigations like these all over the world, but flying squads have also been used domestically in support of FBI field offices temporarily confronted with challenges beyond their capacity to quickly—or as quickly—respond. The beauty of the concept is that it relieves the individual branches and the embassies from keeping larger staffs in case an event occurs that would stress its resources. Paying for staff who would be superfluous under normal conditions does not make sense in an intelligence agency, and it doesn't make sense in a business.

The Business Application of Flying Squads

The concept of corporate flying squads is definitely sound from a logistics standpoint. Mobile human resource teams, able to serve multiple locations, would certainly be more cost-effective than hiring permanent personnel at each branch, who would frankly be superfluous under normal conditions. The cost-effectiveness would benefit both headquarters and the branch. The corporation could make do with less, while the branch would not be burdened with more overhead.

It seems likely that the arrival of a flying squad, or corporate "mobile resource team," would be most welcome at a stumbling point along the critical path of a major project, or during the final steps of preparing a sales bid and presentation to a big customer, or at the outset of a serious workplace crisis. For purposes of illustration, let's consider the application of a flying squad to a sales situation in response to a request from the branch manager.

The branch manager is at her wit's end. Instead of doing what she should be doing—relating on a personal level with her customer counterparts—she is riding herd on a sales team, which is scrambling to get a professional bid package together. The presentation to the customer is only a week away, and the branch manager keenly feels the expectations of senior management. The bid she is preparing represents an order that would be of extreme benefit to the company. She is receiving phone calls every day from the anxious CEO, or one of his surrogates, for a progress report. Never has she been involved in such a high-profile bid. She passes the pressure she is getting down to her sales team, which is working overtime and showing signs of fatigue and irritability. The mood in the office is tense.

The branch manager places the business equivalent of a 911 call and requests from corporate headquarters a mobile resource team. Within two days, a cadre of cool and collected experts enters her office with smiles on their faces, eager to help. The team—completely at her disposal—is composed of specialists. There is a technical guru, who will ensure that the specifications of the bid request have been met in every way and who will be there at the presentation to field the highly specialized questions expected of the customer's IT guru. There is also an audiovisual wizard, who immediately sets to work creating a dynamite presentation, which he will personally run, behind the scenes, at the presentation. A system expert—who knows the product "inside out" and will be on hand to flawlessly demonstrate its features, benefits, and functionality—is part of the team. And, since the presentation will also be videoconferenced to an important sub-sidiary of the customer's in Japan, another flying squad member, a systems expert in his own right, speaks fluent Japanese.

Imagine the relief!

Not only has the flying squad greatly increased the chances of success by its participation, it has taken the burden of sole responsibility off the branch manager in the event the effort fails. It is positively a win-win solution. If the local branch wins the customer contract, victory will be celebrated by all, and if the local branch loses the contract, it will be perceived by corporate that nothing more could have been done—after all, the flying squad was there. A failure, in fact, could just as easily be interpreted as a failure on the part of headquarters, since the flying squad ostensibly represents the corporation at its highest level of management.

There is another, incidental benefit to the flying squad concept: the use of peer pressure as a covert management tool.

The flying squad would be made up of company peers, and peer pressure has always been recognized as a covert tool of management. Even if the entire assistance team is made up of fellow cronies, the branch manager would still want to be at her best before their eyes. And if, as is more likely, there would be one or two strangers on the team, the desire to excel would strengthen. There is no doubt that the presence of top-performing peers keeps us on our toes. The branch manager would, of course, assume leadership of the flying squad, but imagine what that could mean. It would be like leading an FBI SWAT team into action. The burden of leadership would be unbearable unless one was fit enough and tough enough to engender the respect of the fittest and the toughest in the Bureau. In the same way, the branch manager would have to be able to maintain the pace of the flying squad she requested, or suffer the humiliation of raising her hand of "leadership" in exhaustion and call the team to a halt.

The arrival of a flying squad would also have a terrific motivational effect on the branch manager's sales team, which would feel compelled to contribute, if not to show off a bit. And if there were areas of product knowledge in which the salespeople were deficient, they would feel great pressure to "bone up" for the arrival of the flying squad experts.

It should be noted that the magic of peer pressure would work within the flying squad as well. The eyes of the local branch would also be on the experts who have come to their rescue, and there would be a desire to live up to the expectations and to the reputation of the flying squad. Furthermore, the eyes of the members would be on each other! Every member, each chosen for his or her unique skills, would feel a sobering responsibility to contribute to the success of the team. Ask any FBI SWAT member if he does not feel the burden of belonging to that particular brotherhood. What could be worse than feeling like an impostor among earnest specialists?

Considering the benefits of peer pressure, the question arises: Should a flying squad ever be *imposed* on a local branch that is working on a major project?

While the arrival of unrequested assistance could certainly be interpreted as a loss of confidence in the local leadership, it might shake things up a little at the branch in a positive way. A flying squad could be an unofficial wake-up call for a wayward branch manager. Senior leadership could blandly deny there was any question of a loss of confidence in the local branch by claiming, "They were sent to *help* you." But the implicit message would be loud and clear, without all the mess of human resource–oriented evaluation boards or awkward personnel reviews.

The flying squad concept can be a win-win solution, to be sure. But there are serious management issues raised by the implementation of corporate mobile resource teams.

Let's return to the harried branch manager, who is clearly in over her head struggling with a major project and considering asking for a mobile resource team. The prospect of a team of experts coming, like the cavalry, to her assistance is tempting, but would there be second thoughts as she made that 911 call? After all, she is asking for help. Would her ability to manage a major project suddenly be in question? Would she be perceived by her corporate bosses as panicking?

And suppose one of her longtime corporate rivals happened to be on that assistance team? Would her rival use this opportunity to do a little grandstanding at her expense? There are only so many rungs in the corporate ladder. And, although she would be the first to say "we are all on the same team," it is equally true that she and her associates are also in friendly competition for the same managerial or executive positions.

The issue of personal competency aside, what about the feelings of the local sales team members? Would they resent the intrusion of corporate "experts" who swoop in at the last moment to take charge and perhaps to take credit—or at the very least dilute the credit—when the sales team has been immersed in this project from day one? The branch manager knows that the issue of personal "credit" for a successful order is not as petty as it may sound. Salespeople, much like actors, have very strong egos. They struggle for "top billing" in the sales department because a strong personal reputation attracts future plum assignments. When upper management considers to whom it will assign a prestigious account, the most charismatic, successful salesperson immediately comes to mind. So "credit" for previous sales is directly linked to future compensation. If given a choice between winning an important contract single-handedly or as part of a corporate ensemble, any salesperson worth his or her salt will choose the former, especially if his or her commission is negatively affected. "Sharing credit" can often mean "sharing commission."

There is also the opposite case to consider: Suppose the experience with the flying squad is so positive that the sales team would want to repeat it on subsequent projects? Dependency on in-house expertise is often a two-edged sword. A salesperson who looks to others to answer the customer's questions about the product or service does not develop his or her professional capacity. Salespeople in this day and age are supposed to be knowledgeable, if not expert, in their field. If not, how will they spot sales opportunities? Salespeople are also supposed to become leaders who can mentor other salespeople. How will that personal and professional development take place if they depend on flying squads to save their bacon?

Making the Branch Manager Comfortable with Asking for Help

Although it may sound counterintuitive, the best way to make the branch manager comfortable with using a flying squad is to make him pay for it.

The flying squad must belong to the branch for the time it is rendering assistance. That means, for all intents and purposes, the members of the squad must be considered branch employees, under the unqualified direction of the branch manager. It follows, then, that the branch must pick up the tab for these employees and assume all travel and per diem costs of the team members into its overhead. Since branch managers tend to be a very frugal lot, the decision to call the corporate equivalent of 911 would never be taken lightly.

Having to pay for the flying squad discourages indiscriminate use of this valuable corporate resource. The sales team would feel the pinch as well because the money spent would increase branch overhead and reduce commissions. This does away with the branch manager's fears that the sales team will become dependent on the expertise of the flying squad and request its assistance for every other project. The sales team, like the manager, will think twice before dialing 911.

If the corporate response team is a local resource for the time period the assistance is rendered, the branch manager remains in control of his or her project (and of his or her employees on loan). Although they are acknowledged experts, the flying squad members would follow the manager's lead. The outcome would either be a branch victory or a branch defeat (or perhaps a branch stalemate, in which the customer postpones the buying decision). In any case, the flying squad has associated its fate with the local branch. This means, effectively, that the flying squad can never be used as an excuse for a lost deal or for a "successful" deal that turned out to be a loser. Just as the flying squad cannot, as virtual employees of the branch, take unto itself the credit for success, it also cannot be made the scapegoat by the local leadership for failure. After all, during the time of the assistance rendered, the flying squad was part of the branch in every way.

And here's the most important part of being required to pay for the use of a flying squad: Because it is subservient to the branch, the flying squad would not submit a report of its own to corporate leadership. Otherwise, it would be perceived as a mobile board of peer review, and no branch manager in his right mind would ever ask for its help. The flying squad must arrive, in all its glory, to help, not to judge.

Recruiting for Flying Squads

Given the critical role a flying squad can play, should membership be voluntary or assigned?

In its wisdom, the FBI makes membership in the flying squad voluntary. This is also in conformance with its policy for its SWAT and its hostage rescue team (HRT). It would be absurd, for example, to "appoint" someone to be a member of these elite cadres, when membership is open only to those who manage to make it past the gauntlet of obstacles set up to screen out all but the best within the Bureau.

But how does a company make the idea of belonging to a corporate mobile resource team attractive to its already overworked employees, especially if there is no monetary reward for belonging? How does the company answer the perfectly legitimate question of the employee who asks, "What's in it for me?"

Most corporations cannot make an argument for the virtue of self-sacrifice and be taken seriously. If more money is not part of the benefits of belonging to a corporate flying squad, and if the added workload of membership could even jeopardize the current income (for example, sales commissions) of the person considering applying, there have to be compelling reasons for him or her to volunteer. Membership, then, must be considered not only a privilege, but a good career move. While there may not be an immediate monetary award for belonging, it should be clear that membership on the flying squad would be a highlight on the individual's résumé, even a credential recognized throughout the industry, should that person leave the company.

But the prestige of belonging should not be confined to one's résumé. Management should take every opportunity to reference an employee's membership in the flying squad in company biographies, in newsletter articles, and in every introduction. Being a member should be regarded by the rest of the company as a big deal, just as SWAT and HRT—and flying squad—membership is considered prestigious in the FBI. Management can cultivate respect for its mobile resource teams by the way it honors them. Once it is cultivated, a whole new and informal (and cost-free!) layer of management is laid down within the company. That the flying squad would be self-managed in many respects goes without saying. But the effects of its establishment would penetrate deep into the infrastructure. Those who want to belong to a flying squad would learn what it takes to be a member without a supervisor breathing down their neck.

In its evaluation of a flying squad volunteer, management would be wise to look for a history of amenable working relations. Technical experts are, after all, often quite opinionated and intolerant of other perspectives that to them are simply ill informed. They can have thorny personalities. Having worked alone for so long (since nobody else can understand what they're doing), technical gurus sometimes have little appreciation for the importance of teamwork. Most especially, they may have a low opinion, if not outright contempt, for the sales process. Many a deal has collapsed simply because a technical expert took it upon himself or herself to "sell" the product or to display his or her knowledge beyond the scope of the meeting at hand. Many a contract has been lost at the last minute because an expert raised a totally unnecessary rhetorical objection that hadn't even occurred to the prospective customer but that, once articulated, raised unjustified fears.

When it comes to his or her motives, it's certainly acceptable if the flying squad applicant sees membership as a good career move, because it has been so represented by senior leadership. But that cannot be the only or even the primary motive of the volunteer. A career builder will, in all likelihood, not have the self-sacrificial qualities necessary for a good team member and for a good follower. The volunteer would look forward to every squad project as an opportunity to highlight his or her own abilities, which may not always be in sync with the rest of the team's.

Does management want a problem solver who does not feel sufficiently challenged at the home office? Well, yes and maybe no. Flying squad members must be problem solvers, to be sure. But many technical experts have a penchant for perfection. They will obsessively tinker with something long after it has met the required specifications. Imagine the fellow team members drumming their fingers until the perfectionist is satisfied.

Is the volunteer a champion for a specific software program or systems design? If so, he or she may not be open-minded enough to entertain the unthinkable, an alternate program or design offered up by another team member or demanded by the customer.

Is the applicant excited by the prospect of "seeing the world" as a flying squad member? If so, he or she may be sorely disappointed, since very little of the world beyond the walls of the hotel and the customer's conference room will be seen.

Up until now, only company employees have been considered as prospective members of the corporate flying squad, but there are other pools of talent from which to choose. A company could, for example, bring in outside experts from noncompeting organizations—authorities in their field who lend their expertise on a project-by-project basis. Although this option would be more costly, the impact of third-party specialists who stake their reputations on the product, and the company behind the product, can be powerful. Even though the customer would know full well that the experts before them were "hired guns," the customer still might be impressed, reasoning that surely they wouldn't put their professional reputations on the line if they didn't believe in the product.

On the theory that it's always best to keep it in the family, a company could also look to its retirees as potential members of the flying squad, assuming they are still up to speed with the technology being offered. There are several advantages to making use of the company's talented retirees.

First, they are steeped in the company culture, unlike the hired guns, and they are able to comfortably answer every question the customer could throw at them. Second, these articulate, silver-haired former employees would make a positive impression on a prospective customer, who would doubtless be gratified by the vendor's long-term stability in the industry. Third, the retirees are living proof that the vendor has not only been around for a while but that it has cared well for its own employees. The logical conclusion might be that a company that treats its employees well in all likelihood treats its customers well. And finally, there is the confidence-inspiring spectacle of an older generation of employees proudly standing side by side with their replacements, bright-eyed "youngsters" they have personally mentored. We must never forget that every sale is an exchange of trust. The potential customer might warm considerably to the patriarchal and matriarchal presence of former employees who vouch for the vendor and its product or service.

Cross-Training for the Flying Squad Members and Their Support

It almost goes without saying that the establishment of fast-moving, mobile corporate assistance teams presupposes a strong corporate commitment to cross-training. Someone must temporarily replace the departing flying squad member who has rushed out the door leaving his or her work in progress on the desk. Even though the absence of a flying squad member should be fairly brief, someone must be qualified to fill the breach. Since flying squad members are by definition highly talented individuals, their replacements must be up to speed and ready to fill in at a moment's notice while still continuing with their own work. Of course, cross-training is a great idea anyway; employees get the flu, or leave for family emergencies, or go on maternity leave. But for mobile assistance teams to be a workable and long-term corporate resource, a strong training program is not optional. It is essential.

But there is another aspect to cross-training that the FBI does very well. The flying squad member very often spends significant time at the desk of the person he or she will report to.

This is especially important for the agent who must go overseas and who must understand, on nearly a cellular level, the importance of getting timely information back to headquarters so that the FBI Director can have at his fingertips the answers to the questions asked by the President of the United States. In the case (at the time of this writing) of *this* director (Mueller) and *this* president (George W. Bush), it is said that the questions are particularly shrewd and that the Director is "grilled" daily. Woe unto the agent who does not understand the importance of providing the boss with fresh, credible information.

The FBI, in this respect, has instituted a wise and cost-effective policy. Before Special Agent Michael Dehncke joined the flying squad, he was asked to sit at the desk of the person he would be reporting to in Washington, D.C., for *two months*. "Each of us has gone back and sat in the desk of the person we are reporting to," he explains. "We understand their day.

They've got a morning meeting, a midafternoon meeting, and the Director's daily report has to be submitted at a certain time. I know what kind of information is most useful for them, having sat at that desk myself. I also learned, firsthand," he grins, "what it was like to sit in that hot seat and *not* to have the information from the agent in the field on time."

So when agent Dehncke is in some far-flung place—in a nice hotel, or sleeping in a cargo container in the jungle alongside special forces—he gets his report upline on a timely basis. There is no better way of instilling the big picture—or at the very least a bigger picture—than switching places.

Much has been written about the necessity of impressing upon employees the overall scheme of things so that they better understand their contributions to the whole. And companies seem to agree, as evidenced by the pep talks managers give on the subject. But actually plopping someone down in the chair of his counterpart for an extended period of time would probably be considered impractical in most companies. Obviously, the person would have to do more than *sit* at the desk of his associate; he would have to do his associate's job, which means he would have to be taught that job. That is easier said than done, especially if the personality types characteristic of each position are vastly different.

The salesperson in the field, for example, is probably quite a different character than his or her counterpart in order entry. One is a freewheeling extrovert who typically hates paperwork, and the other is a "bean counter" who thrives on detail. Switching places even for a day could be disastrous.

Nevertheless, each has unrealistic expectations of the other. The order entry person wants to know every aspect of the new order. Indeed, her system may be set up so that it will not even process the order until every single piece of the puzzle has been entered. The salesperson, anxious to get his order in before quarter's end, may not even have all the pieces in mind; the deal has been made conceptually. He and his customer have agreed in broad terms and the contract has been signed. The blanks will be filled in when the salesperson can draw a breath.

Both the order entry person and the salesperson are right from their perspectives. It is only when they change places (or at least "ride along" with others in sales and order entry) that their perspectives will broaden in scope and sympathy. Each will learn the difficulties of the other's job as well as the relevant information required to get the ball rolling. Thrown together, the salesperson and the bean counter might even become fast friends who come to respect each other's work rather than be contemptuous of it.

Knowing the big picture is all the more important in the digital age, when more and more responsibilities are off-loaded onto the shoulders of the person who gains the vital information *first*. Administrative support in the "lean and mean" organization is often limited to the provision of a company voice mail system. Less support means fewer people to share the big picture. The customer service rep in the field, for example, can no longer forward her newly gathered information to someone back at headquarters with a computer. *She* has the computer now, in her palm, and is expected to do both jobs. The technology that was supposed to liberate us has made virtual offices of our cars and homes and has added, not subtracted, hours to the business day. It has also made knowing the big picture all the more critical to organizational success. Just because employees are doing more does not mean they understand the impact of their ever-increasing volume of input. The more they know of the scheme of things, the better they will be able to suggest improvements.

It goes without saying that in order to share the big picture, the company culture must be open, not closed. But there are many reasons why a company might want to play its cards close to its vest. If employee turnover is high, senior managers fear having the big picture shared with the competition. Company procedures, in fact, may be proprietary and carefully guarded. Or maybe management doesn't want its employees to have an insight into how overhead is calculated, since it affects everyone's—including the executive's—bonus program. The phrase "it's none of your business" would never be heard in today's polite corporate culture, but it can be instituted into company policy through various safeguards. How many suspense movies have we seen that turn on an inquisitive employee's penetration into company secrets? Do we think for a moment that the execs at Enron wanted to share the big picture?

Providing Logistical Support for the Flying Squad

This is an area in which the business community can learn from the FBI and then go one step further.

While the Bureau, being taxpayer funded, does not especially care for the comfort of its agents on long flights, it does attend to all the other distracting issues associated with international travel.

"In the old days," grins Michael Dehncke, "traveling was the most difficult part of an overseas assignment. There were approvals needed from a hierarchy of departments, reservations to be made, transportation to and from the airports to be set up, overseas paperwork and passports required, and often vaccinations. These are not the things you want to have to worry about when you're trying to get up to speed on the case you're going to be investigating. But nowadays, the Bureau takes care of all of that, so the agent can make more productive use of his or her time."

One might think that every company realizes the importance of freeing the hands and lightening the hearts of employees who must travel on company business, especially in light of the fact that today's business travel experience is much more frustrating than ever before. Today's business emissary must now shuffle, inch by inch, through long lines at the airport terminal's security checkpoints. He or she may have to sit through delays that were unthinkable a decade ago. It has been reported that airline delays in 2007 were the highest they've been in thirteen years. Nearly a quarter of all flights in the first three quarters of 2007 were late. Tens of thousands of flights were canceled. A number of nightmare stories of planeloads of passengers being held on the tarmac for hours were reported. And incidents of passenger rage, unheard of years ago, are now too frequently in the news. The very least the corporation can do in support of its flying squad members is grease the skids logistically by taking care of all the arrangements so the traveling expert can, like the FBI agent, spend his or her time getting up to speed.

But businesses can go one step further and take into consideration the flying comfort of their flying squad. The FBI, being a good steward of taxpayer funds, does not pay for its flying squad members to fly business class. That means six-foot-four Michael Dehncke must find a place for his long legs during the fourteen-hour flight to Asia. He good-naturedly shrugs off the suggestion that he might arrive in a faraway country fresher from a good night's sleep. But surely there is some truth to it.

Jet lag is serious enough that entertainers and professional athletes arrive *days* before the event in which they must be at their best. An FBI agent responding to an overseas crisis cannot include in his schedule the margin of a few days' rest. He must hop on the first available flight. His arrival, furthermore, is highly anticipated by the local law enforcement agencies, who look to him for expertise. Since the first few days after a terrorist bombing are often the most productive in terms of information gathering, the FBI agent usually arrives at a high point of the investigation. All eyes turn to him, for guidance, for leadership. The press demands a statement. Imagine the reaction of the locals if the FBI agent could barely keep his eyes open!

Business travelers are also "on the spot" soon after they arrive in another time zone. They must negotiate a contract, or give an important presentation in front of customers, or help troubleshoot some kind of emergency. Corporate flying squad members, in particular, will have pressing duties by the very nature of their responsibilities. All eyes will turn to them as well.

Yet many businesses persist in regarding business class or first class a scandalous luxury for the corporate soldier. And the idea of sending an employee a couple of days in advance to recover from jet lag is out of the question; it would mean more outlay for hotel rooms and more time away from her regular duties. Not only must the traveling employee fly coach, she is under some frugal corporate policies required to share the hotel room with an associate of the same gender. The upshot is, she can't sleep on the plane and she can't sleep—or sleep well—in the hotel room with someone snoring in the adjacent bed. Exhausted at sunrise, she is nevertheless expected by her organization to be at the top of her game.

If a corporation is going to make the investment required to establish a flying squad of experts who have volunteered to travel at a moment's notice to help secure more business, the least it can do is support them on their way. A good night's sleep is not a luxury; it is a prerequisite for high performance. If the business deal is important enough to send your best and brightest, it is important enough to make sure they are at their best and brightest when they arrive. A seat on the plane in which they can recline and sleep and a five-star hotel in which they can recover from jet lag, if only for a few hours, are basic requirements. But the company can do more.

Arrangements can be made to have hotel staff steam press the suits to be worn later in the day, which have been wrinkled in the suitcase. Videoconferencing facilities can be reserved for a pre-presentation briefing with headquarters. And all important meetings, presentations, or press conferences should be scheduled to accommodate jet lag. This is not pampering; it's simply good business. Not only will the flying squad members perform at their best, they will happily accept the next assignment to a far-off corner of the world.

Of course, the "far-off corner" is a relative concept, defined by time. If an employee takes the red-eye from Chicago to Los Angeles for a presentation that very morning, he should have the benefit of whatever sleep he can get in a fully reclining seat in business class. They don't call it the red-eye for nothing.

Footnote: Flying Squads Are Leadership Pools!

Although every job in the FBI is an important one, not all require the wearing of so many hats. Agent Michael Dehncke and other flying squad members like him very often have to assume, in a foreign country, leadership roles far above their literal job descriptions at home. Dehncke, for example, has facilitated meetings with top government officials. He's been, in effect, an emissary, a diplomat, and a surrogate police chief. Top management at FBI headquarters is not unaware of the job-enhancing duties that often befall a flying squad member. Although Dehncke is loathe to attribute his temporary ascensions into executive positions as "career enhancing" within the FBI, they certainly can't hurt.

Clearly, any business organization would benefit from the personal and professional growth of its flying squad volunteers, who would be faced with leadership-building challenges requiring the utmost in resourcefulness and creativity. Being a member of the corporate mobile resource team would generally cultivate the very skills needed for executive leadership, including customer diplomacy and contract-negotiating skills. Management would doubtless keep a steady eye on each flying squad volunteer as his or her professional capacity increased with each challenge.

Task-Force Management

Supervisory Special Agent (SSA) Kristen von KleinSmid heads the Los Angeles terrorist threat squad. Her office is a hub of activity. The walls are often covered with maps, and the whiteboards beneath them chronicle each update as her team of nine special agents runs down an average of twenty threats per week called in from FBI headquarters, local law enforcement, and concerned citizens. "We get everything," she explains, "from 'My neighbor is a terrorist!' to menacing threats of weapons of mass destruction. No stone is unturned. Each one is checked out, because one of those stones on any given day could be linked to another 9/11."

To keep pace, she personally reads an average of 120 intelligence reports *daily*, any one of which could have direct implications for her domain. Fortunately for the organization, Kristen is one of those people who thrives on four to five hours of sleep. Despite the dizzying amount of activity she must supervise during her long day, she has no problem falling asleep. "When my head hits the pillow," she jokes, "I'm out."

That is, unless the phone rings. Which occurs pretty frequently in the life of a threat squad supervisor.

In the middle of a windy October night, her cell phone vibrated on the bed stand. The Orange County Sheriff's department had just phoned in a lead. A cell phone had been left at a bar, and when the bartender activated the phone to contact its owner, he saw a digital snapshot displayed of a young man dressed in the vest of a suicide bomber girdled with sticks of dynamite.

Kristen looked at the clock. It was 2:46 A.M. Fully awake, she dialed an "all hands on deck" emergency message to her nine agents and the other thirteen members of her local Joint Terrorism Task Force (JTTF), made up of representatives from local law enforcement and state and federal agencies. By 3:00 A.M., twenty-two JTTF members were hot on the investigation.

Within twelve hours, her team had identified the owner of the cell phone and three of his associates. Subpoenas had been granted, and all were being interviewed.

The young man who was the focus of all the attention sat up in his chair and looked at the serious faces of the FBI agents and sheriffs surrounding him. He sheepishly explained that the photo was of his Halloween costume, and the red sticks of dynamite were candles. "Sorry for the confusion," he added lamely.

Kristen was not amused. "His story was checked out and that's exactly what it was. We had an inkling something wasn't right when our explosives expert who examined the photo told us dynamite sticks haven't been the color red in ages. But we took it very seriously as a time-sensitive threat. As it happened, it was a good exercise for our task force."

The FBI's slant on "task-force management" goes well beyond the popular understanding of the term in the business community. When many of us think of task-force management, we probably imagine the business equivalent of the grand strategy rooms of World War II, where admirals and generals used long-handled sticks like croupiers to push miniature ships, planes, and tanks across large charted tables. We naturally think of the modern-day steering committee, composed of senior managers from key departments, putting their heads together to form the company's strategic policy. And that's a good enough definition as far as it goes.

This definition does, however, raise the question, "How many companies actually make use of task-force management principles in this age of the charismatic CEO?" The covers of business magazines feature the full-face portraits of magnetic leaders, not the members of steering committees. Business history, we are to believe, is made by individuals with very strong personalities, not by a board of wise men. There are a number of CEOs today who earn in excess of one hundred million dollars per year in *salary*—including a few at twice that amount—not to mention other forms of compensation like stock options and bonuses. The shareholders aren't complaining; they feel fortunate to have such visionary leaders at the helm.

Indeed the entire corporate chain of command leads to the *captain* of the ship, not to the "leadership committee." And once someone takes on that awesome responsibility and has to make strategic decisions, we are told it is "lonely at the top," which suggests that the CEO plots the course of the company guided mainly by his or her instincts. To the degree to which the CEO has people around, they seem to be not peers but disciples. Very often, the proof that the company has no steering committee is manifested at the departure of the CEO, whose "vision" may have led the company onto the rocks. Why was there no "task force" of wiser heads to prevent this? And, conversely, if the charismatic CEO left the company on a high note and performance subsequently suffers without his or her presence, why was there not a task force in place to continue the strategic course set by the CEO? It's pretty obvious that megacorporations like Enron or WorldCom or Tyco did not have active steering committees of independent-minded department heads with a fiduciary duty to the corporation and with access to any information they required.

The FBI's use of task-force management seems unique in that it applies the task-force concept from the ground up, from the streets of our cities to the global strategy sessions at headquarters. Today, there are JTTFs in more than a hundred cities nationwide. Sixty-five of these JTTFs were created after 9/11 under Director Mueller's mandate. Nationwide, there are nearly four thousand members, roughly half of whom are FBI agents, the rest being local and state law enforcement officers and professionals from a dozen other government agencies (some of which are also mentioned at the beginning of this chapter), such as the DHS, CIA, TSA, CBP, DEA—even the IRS—and members from local fire departments, the district attorney's office, the department of health, the federal prosecutor's office, and other agencies. All these JTTFs report to the National Joint Terrorism Task Force, headquartered in Washington, D.C., which tries to put the puzzle together from all the bits and pieces of information sent upline.

This well-organized task-force structure is used to (a) lever-age the law-enforcement population and even the general popu-lation, and (b) to act as a clearinghouse for information sent upline from all over the globe.

"Ten thousand FBI agents protecting the nation is not a lot," concedes Joe Ford, COO of the FBI. "But through the task-force concept we are leveraging the capabilities of tens of thou-sands of law enforcement agencies and the eyes and ears of hun-dreds of thousands of their officers all over the nation."

The task-force structure also serves as a clearinghouse at the local level. "In Los Angeles, for example," explains Bob Loosle, special agent in charge of the antigang division there, "we have 'LA Clear.' If we're working a drug target, we'll send that name in through LA Clear and they might tell us that no one is work-ing that individual—or the reverse, that the DEA is working him. So then we'll go to the DEA and ask them if we can work a certain angle. They may say OK, or they may want us to hold back a bit because they're just about to bring the enterprise down. Or let's say we want to make a fugitive arrest. We'll call LA Clearance and let them know, and we might be told, 'No problem,' or be told, 'Wait! The marshals are going there too.' So then we'll call the marshals to avoid a blue-on-blue accident from happening."

The effectiveness of any task force is dependent upon all members buying into the concept. Assistant Director Stephen Tidwell remembers a roundtable he once attended with law en-forcement executives from all over the nation. The format was familiar: a facilitator in the middle of the circle coming up with scenarios, then turning quickly on one of the attendees and de-manding an immediate response.

"He created an urgent scenario," recalls Tidwell, "then spun around and pointed his finger at an LAPD exec and said, 'What's the first thing you would do?' The LAPD guy calmly answered, 'I'd pick up the phone and check with the Joint Terrorism Task Force.' He then wheeled around and pointed at an attendee from the district attorney's office and asked him what *he* would do. The DA answered, 'I'd check in with JTTF.' Somewhat deflated, the facilitator turned on me. 'And *you?*' he asked." Tidwell smiles. "I told him I'd check with JTTF before I made another move."

How effective has this system been? The general public may never know of all the successes that can be attributed to the task-force concept. But some examples of the JTTFs in action have been made public, such as the 2001 "Portland Seven" terrorist plot to fight against U.S. troops in Afghanistan, the "Lackawanna Six" plot in 2003 to provide support to a terrorist organization, the 2003 Northern Virginia jihad plot to wage war against America, the 2005 JIS (Jam'iyyat Ul-Islam Is-Saheeh) plot to attack Los Angeles International Airport, the 2007 plan to attack the soldiers at Fort Dix, and the 2007 plot to attack the jet fuel pipeline and supply tanks at JFK International Airport.

The Business Application of Task-Force Leveraging and Clearing

Just as the FBI, with its roughly ten thousand agents, makes use of the eyes and ears of the more than eight hundred thousand law enforcement officers in the nation, so can a business leverage the impressions of its employees, its suppliers, and even its customers, all of whom can be terrific sources of information about developments in the industry and the marketplace. And the business can do it by making the same argument as the FBI's:

Communicating through us is a win-win policy. Just as the FBI persuaded so many other agencies to pass their information up-line to improve their own odds of success, the company can prove to its employees, suppliers, and customers that it is in their own self-interest to communicate without reservation for the betterment of all concerned.

The argument is easiest to make with one's own workforce, which is, of the three legs of the triad, the most dependent on the company. One would think that every employee already realizes that it would be in his or her self-interest to provide the company with information that may be of benefit. And that is probably true in theory. But in practice, if there is no structure to receive (and to solicit) the information, it likely will never make it to the people who can do the most with it.

Let us imagine a service technician who while visiting a major customer notices something that in itself seems curious but certainly not earthshaking: a glazier's truck in the parking lot with a large pane of glass between its racks. The service technician may not deem this observation worth mentioning, or if he does he may make a passing remark to his manager, who is too busy to give it a second thought. Three months later, the CEO storms through the sales department with a business journal in hand reading the highlights of an article describing a sophisticated, hot backup network command center the major customer recently purchased—without so much as a bid from the sales team! As it happened, the service technician had spotted the glazier who had been sent to replace a window after a break-in at the customer's massive computer center, which prompted the customer to install an expensive off-site redundant system. A nice sales opportunity had been lost simply because it had not been recognized.

A favorite rhetorical question asked by CEOs is, "How many

in this room are in sales?" The hoped-for response is that all hands will go up because every employee realizes his or her secondary role as an ambassador of the company. That too may be true in theory but not always in practice. The company has a sales department with a finite number of salespeople. Whatever the number, it is small compared to the employee base, which should be leveraged for all it is worth. A prominent task force, which not only contributes to the strategic thinking of the company but solicits and puts together bits and pieces of information from the workforce, can be a great asset. It can literally wake the employees up to the world (and to the opportunities!) around them. Instead of commuting back and forth on the freeway, listening to music, they can be looking for clues to new business.

Serving as a clearinghouse, the task force can also save the company the embarrassment of having more than one salesperson unknowingly bidding on the same project (and perhaps coming up with differing quotes). This happens too often in large companies with many branches. Not only does simultaneous bidding put the company in an awkward position, it is a waste of time and resources.

Leveraging the eyes and ears of one's suppliers also makes sense. It's a "win" for the company because a number of the leads will turn into business. The supplier wins too by leveraging the company's ability to provide it with new opportunities to serve the company. Major customers also win by communicating to the task force. By giving the vendor a heads-up on a new strategic direction, the customer increases the chances of being served by a company that has "ramped up" for the task.

The larger the customer, the larger the cast of characters required to serve it, and the wider the information-gathering net will be. But our people in the field are busy, with their own job functions and with their own lives. They cannot be depended upon to always recognize the significance of every piece of information that comes their way regarding our customers, suppliers, competition, or the marketplace. Nor can they be relied upon to always pass that information upline, and even if they do, it cannot be assumed that the information will continue on its path to the ears of those who need it. The chance word or fleeting observation that could portend of great things passes by unheeded because the big picture is not sufficiently grasped.

But management does understand the big picture and therefore must involve itself in the information-gathering process by communicating regularly with those in the field. Rumors heard on the street of an impending change of leadership at the customer, or of a new direction in the market the customer is considering, may contain just enough truth to be of vital interest to senior strategists. This is why management must always stimulate acuity in the rank and file. Through phone calls and e-mails and over cups of coffee and lunch, managers have to solicit feedback from the eyes and ears of the organization on a regular basis. Managers have to make sure that the bits and pieces of hearsay and observation having to do with customers, suppliers, competitors, and the marketplace in general are passed upline to those with the big picture in mind. The rank and file, however competent, should not be left to decide what is and is not important.

"Openness" will characterize every successful task force. But the communication should flow both ways. The employees, suppliers, and customers must be kept informed too. Why should the grand corporate strategy be kept a secret from the very people who will implement it where the rubber meets the road? And, for that matter, why shouldn't our suppliers know the specifics of our own corporate vision and how they will fit in? Major customers, certainly, should be involved in plotting the company's course, so that the future can be faced hand in hand. If the strategy eventually becomes known by our competitors, even better; their key players may jump ship. A strategic goal publicly announced has a better chance of being realized. A secret isolates energy, but once shared, the open declaration draws support from all kinds of sympathetic sources.

Case in point: In the aftermath of 9/11, FBI Director Robert Mueller announced to Congress and to the world the creation of the National Joint Terrorism Task Force. But why announce it publicly? The establishment of the NJTTF could have been described to Congress in a closed-door session. The public would have understood the natural reticence of the FBI to expose its response to the terrorist threat. Fighting terror is, after all, a secretive business. But Director Mueller made his dramatic reorganization public. And by doing so he sent a message to his employees, to his "customers," and to his "competition."

By announcing the new priorities of the agency, Mueller put his agents on notice in the most public way and thereby enlisted the public as an informal layer of "management."

He also told his customers, the American people, what they could expect of the FBI, which is tantamount to inviting them to hold the agency accountable. He also enlisted the vigilance of the public, further leveraging his finite resources.

And he, in essence, openly declared war on his competition. By doing so publicly, he put himself and his agency in a do-or-die situation. A commitment broadcast to the entire world has far more impact than one announced behind closed doors. Once the goal is broadcast, the reputation of the organization is on the line. There is a nonnegotiable, unconditional-victory aspect to the stance taken. More importantly, the terrorists are forced to confront a frightening consequence of their actions—the FBI has declared war on them. Surely some of even the most fanatical proponents of terror do not sleep well with that realization and may even opt out of the cause.

Taking Every Threat Seriously

It is noteworthy that the JTTF takes every threat seriously and that threat squad supervisor Kristen von KleinSmid leaves "no stone unturned" in her validation of each warning. Her "all hands on deck" response to what turned out to be a Halloween costume is instructive for all of us in the business community. It would have been easy for her to downgrade the level of that specific threat the moment her explosives expert cast doubt on the sticks of dynamite. To her credit, she never let up. Although sticks of dynamite haven't been red for decades, she acted on the assumption that they were sticks of some kind of explosive and that the lives of innocents were at imminent risk.

Her attitude reflects a humility that serves the FBI and the general public well. With all the resources at her disposal, it might be tempting to regard certain types of threats as so disproportionate to the power of the federal government as to be almost laughable. The odds that a phone call from a little old lady who believes that her neighbor is a terrorist represents a threat to the nation must be admittedly small. Nonetheless, Kristen's threat squad—and others like it all over the country—take each threat seriously.

In other words, they do not look down on the "competition." And neither should we.

The irony of having great pride in the organization we serve—of being conscious, for example, of working for the industry leader—is that we may not recognize the very real threat posed by a comparatively insignificant competitor. The parable of IBM underestimating the threat posed by college whiz kids like Steve Jobs and Bill Gates, who were developing the "computer for the rest of us" in their garages, is usually invoked to warn against the business sin of arrogance. And certainly it's a great lesson. But since product revolutions don't happen every day, it might be useful to look at a more common consequence of even justified pride.

A company sales representative, for example, who believes so strongly in the superiority of her product and in the unassailable leadership position of the organization she serves is apt not to recognize her competitors, in a bidding situation, as legitimate peers. Inadvertently, her uncompromising attitude allows her company to be cast in the customer's mind as Goliath and enables her earnest competitor to be David. Worse yet, she implies, through her unshakeable confidence, that the customer cannot differentiate between pale imitations and the real thing.

By appearing to take every threat seriously, we are letting our customer know that we do not take him or his business for granted. We are showing the kind of humility customers like to see in every supplier or contractor, especially the larger ones. Although we may be a Goliath in resources, we must always remain a David in attitude.

CHAPTER SIX

Managing the Highly Motivated

Cultivate good cheer • Establish an awards board of former
recipients • The importance of budget to performance
• The appeal to self-sacrifice

It's great to work in an organization where everyone
thinks it's an honor to belong.

—SPECIAL AGENT JEFF GREEN, LEADERSHIP SCHOOL, FBI ACADEMY

Consider for a moment the kind of workforce the FBI manager
must supervise. Every employee is a survivor of a screening process that weeds out 90 percent of tens of thousands of applicants every year. All were about thirty years old when they
applied for the job. All were chosen, in part, for their records of
achievement in civilian life. All have college degrees. All are,
furthermore, graduates of the FBI Academy. Most have been
put through advanced leadership/management courses through-

out their careers. Most have taken a pay cut just to belong to the organization.

We should all be so lucky!

With such a workforce, the managerial "challenges" are often the reverse of those encountered in the business community. Instead of cracking the whip to increase production, field supervisors often find themselves telling their agents to go home and get some sleep. Rather than searching for volunteers, they must choose from a roomful of raised hands. Instead of assigning difficult cases to individual agents, the agents often bring the cases to them and ask for permission to begin an investigation that may involve risk of life and limb. And rather than having to "pump up" the rank and file with inspirational pep talks, they are humbled by the indefatigable commitment throughout the organization.

Nonetheless, the management principles used in support of the natural exuberance of the street agent have significance for all of us in the business community concerned with cultivating and maintaining higher levels of performance.

Cultivate Good Cheer

A career in law enforcement, and in the FBI specifically, has emotional challenges above and beyond those faced by the rest of us. The work, by its very nature, offers little psychological shelter. FBI agents are exposed to an incessant bombardment of negative karma: murderers; kidnappers; hate-filled terrorists; vicious gangbangers; serial killers; pedophiles; and all other manifestations of human greed, depravity, and fanaticism. For most citizens, the workplace offers a distraction from the evil that men do, but for the agent, the office is the focal point of society's organized defense against that evil. There is no effort to disguise that fact in the Los Angeles field office. Through the lobby, the agent passes by the black-and-white photographs on the wall of the faces of dozens of FBI agents killed in action. In the office proper, there is a plaque presented in a tearful ceremony by the parents of little Samantha Runnion, who was kidnapped and murdered despite the sleepless efforts of the FBI agents who led the investigation. Inside the desks and filing cabinets are the crime scene photos of other innocent victims of all ages and from all walks of life.

In addition to these graphic reminders of the nature of their work, there is the unrelenting stress. How would *you* like to bear the primary responsibility for preventing a weapons of mass destruction attack on an American city, or the next murder of an elusive serial killer, or a drug shipment that can ruin the lives of hundreds after its dispersal? In fact, most of the FBI's investigations are a race against time. The term "drop-dead deadline" has literal meaning for agents chasing down an anonymous bioterrorist threat or trying to narrow in on the location of a sadistic kidnapper. In the midst of these kinds of investigations, sleep is hard to come by, nutrition is a running joke, healthy exercise is an impossibility, and the joys of family life are put on hold. Even victory, when it comes, can be short-lived when criminals occasionally walk freely out of the courtroom on a technicality or when scores of masked volunteers clamor to take the place of a captured terrorist. And sometimes, sad to say, there is a lack of public support, as expressed in cynical media coverage and even in congressional legislative proposals that would make the FBI's job even more difficult.

Why, then, are so many FBI agents fundamentally cheerful professionals who love their jobs?

"It's a fun job" is something one hears from agents so frequently that, although anecdotal, it seems statistically to be a widespread sentiment. Backing up this impression is the exceptionally low turnover rate of Bureau personnel (4.7 percent) compared to other federal agencies (6.6 percent), and that includes the mandatory retirements of FBI agents at age 57, which is much younger than in other federal agencies.

The innate good cheer of actual FBI agents certainly doesn't jibe with the Hollywood portrayals of stressed-out, tight-lipped men and women whose only emotional release is the occasional outburst against the restrictions imposed on them by headquarters. But wouldn't it be a contradiction in terms for the FBI to be a repressed organization simmering with discontent, *and* simultaneously successful?

It is simply not possible to hate your job and do it well for any length of time, and certainly not over a twenty-five-year career. The FBI is one hundred years old. If its agents were as portrayed on film, the organization would not have persevered beyond a generation of employees, much less would it have a record of such distinction that the very idea of being investigated by the FBI sends shivers along the spines of criminals and corrupt public officials alike. Furthermore, if FBI agents loved their work less than the Mafioso, the Mafia would have won! Common sense and life experience tell us that, everything else being equal, those who enjoy their jobs outperform their competitors who do not.

Cheerfulness and morale are similar, but they are not synonymous. Historians agree that the German army in World War II had high morale (at least initially); patriotic fervor went so deep as to border on fanaticism. The German military band music, with its swelling, almost symphonic, hymns to the Fatherland, invoked the spirit of self-sacrifice within the rank and file. In contrast, the gum-chewing American GI wanted to live, as he tapped his toes to Major Glenn Miller's upbeat renditions of "The Saint Louis Blues March," "American Patrol," "Jeep Jockey Jump," and "G.I. Jive." While both sides had plenty of morale, the less indoctrinated GI was demonstrably more cheerful. The same might be said of the national leaders in opposition during that momentous conflict. The forever smiling and confident FDR certainly projected a different image than his stern, serious counterparts in the Axis alliance.

This applies as well to private enterprise. A cheerful workplace is almost always a reflection of management. And it is the irony of ironies that so many managers assume a gravitas that is both out of character (if you really got to know them) and counterproductive in terms of its effect on others. They want to be perceived as stoically shouldering the burdens of the marketplace as they pass through the open cubicle area to a closed-door meeting, where, we are to presume, weighty decisions are to be made involving the fate of the company. Managers must fear that to be seen whistling a carefree tune on the way to the boardroom would diminish the dignity of office and our opinions of them. And, unfortunately, they may be right. It seems as if cheerful people are not taken as seriously as their frowning, contemplative counterparts. It's as if we feel that the outwardly lighthearted have not yet come to grips with reality, and once they have, their serious demeanor will signify that they have made the rite of passage into "adulthood."

Consequently, aspiring managers mimic their no-nonsense superiors. Members of the rank and file want to demonstrate to their grave supervisors that they, too, understand the serious nature of the challenges facing the company, so they also walk around in great seriousness. In this way management dampens the natural exuberance of the workforce. Instead of laughter, there is commitment. Instead of smiles, one sees determination. Instead of occasional lapses of routine, there is unceasing production—until the day comes when the seriousness ethos can no longer be sustained and the incidences of sick leave from psychic exhaustion jump and costly employee turnover increases.

Surely few jobs are as weighty as that of an FBI agent, yet they seem to be a cheerful, well-adjusted, mentally healthy lot. Part of that, reasons Special Agent in Charge (SAC) Steve Martinez, has to do with expectations. "We hire people who realize this isn't a nine-to-five job and that there will be lots of challenges. We knew what we were getting into when we chose this line of work. But the Bureau is proactive in areas where we know there are particular vulnerabilities."

An example of the FBI's proactive approach would be its overwatch of the cyber-crime agents investigating child pornography rings on the Internet. "These agents see some horrendous images. We have a program where a psychologist looks deep into their eyes every six months just to make sure the work isn't getting to them. But there are always cases for every agent that can be particularly tough, like kidnappings."

Steve worked the Samantha Runnion investigation out of the Los Angeles office. Like all kidnappings, the investigation was intense. Agents worked round the clock to find and rescue the little girl. While by far the vast majority of kidnappings are happily resolved by the FBI, this one was not. Capturing the suspect days later seemed almost a hollow victory for the exhausted agents on the case. Parents themselves, everyone in the office shared the grief of Samantha's mother at the dedication ceremony out on the grass in front of the federal building. Few were able to keep their composure as the mother spoke, and few tried. "It's not always possible to steel yourself to the things you see, and to the outcomes of some investigations," Steve reveals. "Many tears fell that sad morning."

As the executive in charge of the Las Vegas office, Steve does his best to cultivate a cheerful workplace. "The danger for me in this office," he jokes, "is not to gain forty pounds from all the things people bring in on a regular basis. We had a birthday party last week for one of our folks and there must have been thirty people crowded in her office—from SWAT, organized crime, and the antiterror squads—giving her cards and passing the cake around. And that's a typical scene in a functioning FBI office."

Steve Martinez's office has a volunteer recreation association that plans picnics and family events for the agents and their families. "As a SAC [branch exec] I have to be way out front in promoting those kinds of events. I want to be present at every one to show that it's important to me too. I'll bring my wife so everyone knows my family is just as supportive." Halloween is a good example of this executive's philosophy of having fun when you can. "We invite the families, so of course the kids are in their costumes and they trick or treat throughout the office. Don't tell the Director," he jokes, "but when they get to my office, they see a guy in a suit behind the desk, wearing a pair of oversized novelty sunglasses and looking pretty ridiculous."

In a heartbeat, SAC Steve Martinez can put on his game face and lead a task force of street agents, crusty old-time sheriffs, tough cops, and hard-boiled police detectives into the fray. But he recognizes the need for balance in the workplace, and he knows from experience that "cheerfulness" in the rank and file is a management issue.

There is a variation on this theme of maintaining cheerfulness that should be considered: There are times when a manager should allow his or her subordinates to grieve—at least temporarily—over a job-related failure.

In talking to a number of FBI agents, one gets the definite impression that they take their work personally, as opposed to philosophically. When Steve Martinez and his fellow agents stood on the grass in front of the federal building for the memorial ceremony for little Samantha Runnion, they could have comforted themselves with the statistics of the Bureau's success at happily resolving cases of child abduction. By far, most kidnapping cases are successfully concluded. And even in the case of Samantha, there was the silver lining of catching the man responsible for her death and thus preventing more crimes against children. The agents could have put this one case—this one tragic case—in perspective, up against a thousand other happy endings. Instead they either blinked back tears or wept openly.

In moments like these, perhaps the best thing a manager can do is let the agents pass through their spells of grief toward a renewed determination to fight all the harder the next time a child is kidnapped. Trying to cheer people up at that moment would be to deny them the healing opportunity to increase their resolve. It would be counterproductive, because top performers always personalize defeat.

In the business environment, many of us take success personally and defeat philosophically. A salesperson who brings in a large contract attributes his success to his own abilities—as an active listener who understood the needs of the customer better than the customer did, and as a creative problem solver who provided a solution to the customer none of his competitors could come up with. But when that same salesperson loses a major contract, he attributes his failure to outside forces, such as his company's inability to meet the customer's needs with the right product or the noncompetitive pricing structure he is forced to work with. If by some chance he does blame himself, his manager should allow him to do so, at least for a while, rather than rush over to pat him on the back and put his defeat in perspective with some kind of variation of "You can't win 'em all" or "Don't forget that Barry Bonds, the home run king, struck out 1,539 times."

The manager who allows his or her top performers to occasionally go through the "dark night of the soul," as they try to figure out the possible causes of a significant failure, will be doing them a favor, for the top performer will emerge from that introspective process cleansed, renewed, and ready to do better the next time. To allow employees to treat defeat philosophically rather than personally is to allow them to diminish, in their own minds, their personal power to overcome the obstacles to success.

Another way to cultivate good cheer is to award agents for good work.

Establish an Awards Board of Former Recipients

Street agent Craig Arnold retired in 2005 as the FBI's most decorated agent. He was awarded the Bureau's highest honor, the Medal of Valor, for breaking through a motel door at the sound of gunfire and killing, in self-defense, the drug dealer who had just shot a cooperating witness. He won the coveted Shield of Bravery for driving his car into a gunfight and smashing into a carload of kidnappers who were trying to escape with their hostage. He won yet another Shield of Bravery for busting into a warehouse with his SWAT team and capturing a terrorist cell in the process of filling fifty-gallon drums with high explosives. And he was awarded the FBI Director's Award for Criminal Investigation. In each case, it wasn't so much the medal that humbled him; it was being selected for it by the very agents he had admired for years.

Although these decorations were bestowed upon him with much ceremony by senior management, senior management had no role in selecting him. Instead, Craig was singled out for recognition by the FBI's Medals Board, which is composed of only two special agents in charge from the field and two "street" agents who have been awarded the Medal of Valor. Since the Bureau's highest honor is bestowed sparingly, the board is necessarily small. It meets periodically to consider and vote upon recommendations that come in from the field for valor, bravery, and meritorious achievement.

"The FBI gets this right," believes Craig. "To be a member on the Medals Board as a field agent, you have to have been a recipient of the Medal of Valor. No FBI headquarters bureaucrats are involved in the decision-making process unless there is a tie between the four members. But it is basically a matter of street agents recognizing the valor and bravery of other street agents. FBI headquarters management stays out of it."

One can hardly say that in most companies management "stays out of" the various employee recognition programs, such as employee of the month, salesperson of the year, customer service award, and special achievement award. On the contrary, management initiates the selection and presides over the presentation of its corporate "medals." Although management's intentions are good and although the recipients surely must feel honored, the corporate awards system may be significantly improved by emulating the FBI's selection process.

Because recognition from one's peers, top performers all, is even more special.

Consider the possible negatives the FBI has eliminated from its medals program by keeping "corporate" out of it. There is no politicking, no favoritism, no question of nepotism, no impression given of "career-building" awards arbitrarily given to employees targeted for promotion, no backlash from the rank and file, and no diminishment of previous awards. Furthermore, senior management has been relieved of the awful burden of having to choose between deserving subordinates.

The very fact that the medals have been awarded by previous recipients ends all speculation on the part of the rank and file. For who could be a sterner judge? How many NFL football players would be comfortable in allowing only Hall of Famers to select future members? Probably a great many players would prefer that less exacting judges—the sportswriters and the fans—continue to make the decisions. But imagine the pride of being selected by those who have earned the honor themselves! To take an example from World War II, it would mean the difference between receiving the Congressional Medal of Honor from Sergeant Audie Murphy or from Franklin Delano Roosevelt. The president, bless him, would have been in no position to evaluate what constituted extraordinary performance on the battlefield.

By empowering the highest-decorated street agents to determine who shall receive the Bureau's highest honor, senior management is tacitly acknowledging that it is not in the best position to make this call. Corporate leaders might do well to make that admission and to allow their top performers to identify and reward those who have accomplished what they have. They certainly would know best. They could determine, from experience, truly exemplary behavior. For example, when considering two candidates for the salesperson of the year award, someone who has "been there and done that" would be able to read the story behind the press release and look behind the numbers. One contender for the award, for example, may have inherited a large order or have had a "bluebird" land on her desk, while the other—whose numbers might be less—might have brought in a new and highly coveted customer after months of hard work.

On the subject of awards, it should be remembered that the FBI, like the military, is more interested in valorous behavior than in the outcome of that behavior. Sometimes, tragically, the outcome is not a "success" in the way the business world might define it. Medals, for example, are sometimes awarded posthumously to an agent who sacrificed his or her life so that others might succeed. Awards in the business community are associated with successful achievement, but it might make sense to also consider a "best assist" award. Just as a basketball player can, with an ingenious pass, enable a teammate to score, an account rep who fails to get a major contract may nonetheless have made significant positive inroads on the customer so that the next sale is consummated by one of her associates. The original salesperson "failed" in a literal sense but made success possible for her company. By awarding her for her efforts, management encourages the fighting spirit and sends the message that it understands and appreciates the long-term consequences of the hard work of its employees.

One of the benefits of having an awards board made up of top-performing peers is that it creates a desire to sit at the "roundtable" oneself—and to therefore earn that right. When Craig Arnold was asked to be on the Medals Board, he didn't know what was more humbling, receiving the Medal of Valor or sitting in the chair of vacating board member Special Agent Ed Mireles, the hero of the Miami Dade County shoot-out. "It was an honor to replace Ed Mireles on the board because in my eyes and in the eyes of all who knew of his actions, he was a true FBI hero. It was absolutely awe inspiring to take his seat." When members of any organization unabashedly admire those who have performed above and beyond the call of duty, there is no need for management to further motivate. They have been sufficiently inspired to enter, one day, a select membership of top-performing peers—subsidized by management as a kind of absentee landlord.

One of the keys to engendering the admiration of fellow employees is to always retain the "currency" of the awards. As important as whom to recognize for valorous behavior is whom not to recognize. Craig Arnold keenly felt his responsibility to maintain the value of the Medal of Valor and Shield of Bravery. "My selection to the board was an honor," he recalls. "I felt like I was a guardian of all those who had come before me, most especially Special Agent Mireles. I was responsible for ensuring that brave deeds of past recipients were not diminished by the lessening of standards."

There are essentially two ways of diminishing the value of coveted company awards: first, by bestowing the honor on someone who has not met the standards set by previous recipients, and second, by creating an even higher award.

The first is easily understood. If the boss's son is arbitrarily presented with an award he is obviously not entitled to receive, the honor of that particular award has been lessened for all past and future recipients.

The second and unintentional diminishment occurs when management creates a new, higher category of achievement. Many companies have an equivalent of a President's Club or Silver Circle, which honors their top performers in sales, customer service, marketing, production, etc. Recognized throughout the organization as the apex of performance recognition, membership is coveted and proudly displayed with lapel pins or company rings by those who have entered these exclusive circles. But when a company, in a misguided attempt to spur performance to even greater heights, creates yet another, loftier plateau of recognition—some kind of super-duper Silver Circle—it diminishes the honor previously bestowed. Just imagine if the FBI "updated" the criteria for its coveted Medal of Valor and added another category for the really *really* valorous, or if the Baseball Hall of Fame opened a modern annex called the Baseball Hall of Even Greater Fame. To do so would bring into question the achievements of the earlier recipients. Yet some companies blithely institute their own versions of these silly examples. A better way to recognize "higher" performance would be to simply include a bonus. Everyone knows that Babe Ruth made less money than Mark McGwire, yet the Baseball Hall of Fame, like heaven, is populated with equals. One of the fastest ways management can lower morale is by diminishing past performance in an effort to inspire current productivity.

One last note on the awarding of honors: Hollywood gets this right. Part of the pleasure of watching the Academy Awards ceremony is experiencing the suspense. Within every award category, each nominee is recognized and the work of each nominee is presented, in encapsulated form, to the audience. Only then is the winner announced. It's not surprising, with so many film directors around, that Hollywood knows how to sustain the thrill of anticipation. But by showing samples of the creative genius of each nominee, the winner's achievement is put in context and seems all the more remarkable for the competition. If the master of ceremonies were to simply walk on stage, make the announcement, and present the Oscar, we would never fully appreciate the triumph of the honoree nor would we appreciate all the other great talents at work within the industry.

Craig Arnold, in fact, enjoyed being on the Medals Board for precisely this reason. "I got to read about all the actions that had taken place all over the world in which FBI agents acted with great courage. It was not only inspiring, it was instructive. I had the benefit of the experience of other agents that I would apply to my own SWAT team preparation and training."

An awards ceremony for a company's top performers should be not only inspiring, but instructive. By recognizing all the "nominees" and by illustrating the resourceful and proactive work of each with a little vignette, management can show that the bright path toward achievement has many points of origin. Furthermore, the audience will be comforted and inspired by the fact that there is more than one hero striving on the company's behalf.

Don't Forget to Recognize the "Other Half" of the Workforce

When it comes to awards ceremonies, every company would do well to follow the FBI's example of recognizing the spouses of those being honored on the platform.

Matt Heron, in his twenty-two years with the Bureau, has presided over many awards ceremonies. "Generally," he says, "I'm sitting there on the stage with a good view of the audience. When the agent is getting his or her award, I'll watch the wife or husband and the rest of the family in the audience. I can see the tears of pride. And I'll make a point of going up to them afterwards and thanking them for *their* sacrifice."

FBI execs and supervisors are acutely aware of the supporting role of the "other half" of the workforce. The wife of an agent, for example, must put up with a lot. Her husband often works wild and unpredictable hours and occasionally is nowhere to be found at the children's soccer games and birthdays. Although he cannot share the details of his work, she knows there is the element of physical danger. She may have even attended the funerals of fallen agents.

Retired agent Jack García thanks his lucky stars for the support of his wife. "The undercover agent is not only in some scary situations, but he has to adopt different lifestyles. Sometimes I'd come home dressed like a wise guy; the next day I looked like a dope dealer. One of the roles I played, as I infiltrated the Mob in New York City, was the owner of a strip club. You need an understanding wife for that one!"

And it must be remembered that the spouse is also well aware that the FBI husband or wife can make a lot more money in private enterprise, as an attorney or accountant or executive, without the impossible hours and without being shot at. The spouse shares the pillow, and has the ear, of that FBI agent. If he or she is not "on board" with the agent's chosen calling, there can be problems.

But is it all that different in corporate America? Executives and managers work ungodly hours too, and they miss their share of quality family time. If the company takes the "other half" of the workforce for granted, it can be in for an unpleasant surprise. Every opportunity should be taken to thank the spouses for their support and to educate them on the importance of the work the employee husband or wife is doing. An occasional bouquet of flowers with a handwritten note of thanks from the CEO would not be a bad idea, either, after a particularly stressful project. Because, chances are some of that stress followed the employee home.

The Importance of Budget to Performance

Undercover agent Jack García, during his twenty-six years with the Bureau, lived with uncertainty. He never knew if or when his true identity might be discovered by the drug cartel or by the organized crime family he had infiltrated. When he walked into a restaurant with a cadre of wise guys, he was unsure whether or not he would walk back out. His life might be in danger even if—especially if—they believed his cover; bad guys double-cross each other all the time, for drugs, for money, and for power. And it was often unclear where his investigations would ultimately lead. But he was sure of one thing: Each investigation had a budget associated with it before it began.

"We always knew the budget up front for each investigation. That budget is set aside; it's case-specific. Funding would cover, for example, vehicles, telephones, technical gear, an apartment or an office, expenses, entertainment—everything you need to play your role convincingly. You can't pretend to be a Wall Street broker and not even have an office. The money is spent very wisely, and approvals have to go through all the channels as the money is being spent. But it's a great feeling to know the budget has been committed by the Bureau for that particular case."

In the business environment, money is always a touchy subject. When the topic arises in friendly conversation, it is by mutual consent restricted to its most general terms. One of the greatest breaches of social etiquette is to ask someone how much money he or she makes. It is a difficult enough topic when it is truly relevant, such as during a job interview. The candidate may be in total command during the interview, but reluctant to appear overly concerned with the money. The "salary question" is often, in fact, postponed until the final few moments, and then raised by the candidate almost apologetically, as if it were an impertinence. Later, at home with her husband, she can re-create the entire interview, pointing out her brilliant responses here and there, but when asked for specific details of money matters—salary, bonus, vacation policy, benefits, health care, etc.—she cannot recollect the details.

Managers are well aware of the natural reluctance on the part of their employees to discuss money issues and will put on a quizzical face whenever the topic is raised, as if puzzled by the relevance of the issue of money to workplace matters. Money is, of course, related to performance in the form of a reward (bonus, raise in salary, or promotion), but almost never as a pre-requisite for performance. When we are presented with a challenging assignment, such as a major project or a sizeable sales quota, management is ready to answer most of our questions, but it does not expect us to ask for more money—in the form of corporate resources dedicated to the challenge—to get the job done. Nor would many of us have the temerity to request it. The challenge offered us is supposed to be met with personal initiative, grit, and work ethic. "And you're just the guy to do it," they assure us, with slaps on the back and hearty platitudes like "Go get 'em, tiger."

But budget has everything to do with performance in every other endeavor in life. A well-known military tactic is to cut off supplies to the enemy to degrade his performance; the most fanatical force will find it difficult to succeed when there is no fuel for the tanks, ammunition for the rifles, or meal rations for the soldiers. Professional athletes are absolutely pampered between intense workout sessions—with the best of everything in the way of accommodations, nutrition, physical therapy—because the coaches and the team owners want them to perform at their best. Conversely, critically acclaimed Broadway plays close down for lack of funds, not for lack of talent. Innovative products never "take off" simply because of marketing on the cheap. Even the all-powerful federal government cannot operate without a budget, as we taxpayers are occasionally reminded by threats of a shutdown during a congressional funding crisis.

If budget is critical to the macroperformance of a company, why wouldn't it be proportionately critical to microperformance? Every assignment passed down from management should have the explicit and demonstrable commitment of the company. Words are not enough. An employee challenged with a substantial goal is entitled to see management "put its money where its mouth is" by providing the tools necessary for the successful achievement of that goal. Experienced project managers and veteran salespeople know this. It is the neophyte who generally accepts that "mission impossible" from management without asking for more.

FBI management by allocating a budget to each investigation is partnering in one of the few ways it can with the agent. It is as if the "organization" were walking shoulder to shoulder with the street agent into battle. This practical gesture would be appreciated by all field representatives in private enterprise; they would know that their company is with them on difficult and often lonely assignments.

When budget is limited and simply cannot be supplemented so that it is proportionate to the task, management must chip in with creative ideas to accomplish the goal without the necessary resources.

An example of budgetary limitations being the mother of invention was a case code-named Royal Charm, which began as a local investigation and soon expanded to global proportions. Undercover agent Tom Zyckowski spent six years on this case as a fairly uncomplicated stolen goods scheme revealed itself to be part of a vast money-laundering, weapons-trafficking, and narcotics-smuggling conspiracy. "The challenge," reveals Tom, "was to get all the bad guys, from Asia and Europe and from both coasts of the U.S., in one place at one time where they could be arrested."

Everybody on the squad working the case put their heads together and came up with a cost-effective solution. It was decided that two undercover agents who had posed as lovers during the investigation would get "married." Beautifully embossed wedding invitations were sent to the masterminds of the global criminal enterprise on three continents, along with the printouts of reservations made in "the lovers'" name at a posh casino/hotel. So credible had been the performance of the undercover agents on this prolonged investigation that the international kingpins accepted! They arrived bearing outrageously expensive wedding presents and checked into their posh hotel suites. "The day of the wedding," concludes Tom, "we sent limousines around to pick them up—and arrested the lot of them."

While the "lack of budget" should never be cynically invented as an excuse to spur creativity, there are times when it can do just that. The key to retaining employee confidence is the earnest involvement of management in the search for a solution. Generally speaking, though, adequate budget—equal to the assigned task—is a prerequisite to success.

The Appeal to Self-Sacrifice

In today's upwardly mobile society, it may come as a surprise that a great number of FBI agents have taken pay cuts—in some cases significant pay cuts—to join the Bureau. Physicians, attorneys, accountants, information technology officers, and other professionals in high demand know full well that their earnings as FBI agents have been capped at a level far below those similarly qualified on the outside.

Not only will they make less money as FBI agents, they will work harder, longer, and under a considerably greater sense of urgency. For less money, they will work through weekends and often away from their families. For less money, they will endure discomfort and physical danger. And for less money, they will serve an organization in which, and for which, some of their predecessors have been killed in gun battles. Contrary to all the wisdom of the popular culture, and in opposition to all the advice of the gurus in the business magazines, they will voluntarily *lower* their own standards of living to belong to an organization that can never match the salaries and perks left behind in private enterprise.

Of course, the FBI has its own "competitive advantage" when it comes to recruiting these high-level professionals, such as the opportunity to serve one's country and to defend the innocent. Few corporations can credibly invoke such high purpose. But it is possible for a company to emulate, to some small degree, the FBI's appeal to self-sacrifice.

It begins with a reassessment of today's employee pool of college graduates. Young adults today are looked upon by marketers as belonging to perhaps the savviest generation ever spawned—highly intelligent and not about to be fooled. With unprecedented resources at their fingertips (Internet forums and blogs, chat rooms, electronic bulletin boards, etc.), their eyes are wide open to alternative career paths, employment opportunities, and prevailing compensation standards. Judging by the advertising campaigns targeting this generation, material goods are of prime importance, not only for the pleasure they offer, but for the nearly obsessive need to be on the cutting edge of consumer capability. This is why new digital products (iPods, cell phones, games, cameras, etc.) offering some new increment of personal power are in such unceasing demand even though they may be only slightly tweaked over previous rollouts. Concomitant with this market awareness is a presumed enlightened self-interest that can be satisfied only by similar "leading-edge" offerings from the job market.

But there definitely are circumstances when even the savvy will willingly forgo a more lucrative offer. If, for example, a company were to be known as the undisputed leader in its particular industry, one might consider working there for less. Or if a company's training program were to be recognized as an industry credential, valued by every other organization in the business, one might turn down other more lucrative offers for the opportunity to learn from the best. Or if a startup company were to be on the leading edge of a new and exciting technology, or a pioneer into an uncharted market, it might very well attract exceptionally talented people who respond to the challenge—and not necessarily to the compensation packages of the megacorporations in the same industry.

There are in fact many examples of capable young men and women right out of college who voluntarily choose an employer that pays less, for the exciting opportunity offered. For example, given the choice between working for an innovative biotech company on the front lines of the greatest medical challenges of the century, such as AIDS or cancer, and working for a giant pharmaceutical firm in the process of developing a new, "improved" shampoo formula that "leaves hair soft to the touch," grad students in biology often will go with the smaller company even though the salary and the benefits are considerably less. And there are attorneys on the city payroll who spend their entire careers prosecuting criminals when they could have made ten times the money by defending them. And there are those who choose to remain "in the family" with a smaller company for less money rather than accept an offer from a large conglomerate where the employees scarcely know each other's names.

So it certainly is possible for a company to stay out of the bidding war for new talent and to unapologetically offer the opportunity for meaningful and exciting work without trying to match the competitor's compensation package. But in order to be credible, the company must make use of its top performers as recruiters instead of subbing out this crucial responsibility to headhunting firms. When a candidate for the FBI is interviewed by a team of street agents, he knows he is in the presence of the real thing.

The desire of Generation X to serve a great cause is much stronger than the advertisers realize, as evidenced by the passionate involvement of college students in political campaigns and in social movements. A company recruiter has every right to point out to the prospective candidate the corporate vision for a better world—its ecofriendly energy policies, its scrupulous recycling program, its sponsorship of meaningful community development projects, its history of volunteerism. These spiritual "perks" should not be discounted. Coupled with the contagious passion of the recruiter, who is a top performer and true believer, the company's record of corporate citizenship can be credibly presented as part of the compensation package, and it can mean as much to the sincere applicants as the company car, the Blackberry, and the vacation policy.

FBI agents are justifiably proud of their organization, but there is no reason why a company in private enterprise cannot cultivate a similar sense of self-esteem in its own employees. This is no time for modesty. Management should communicate the company's record of achievement to all—and often.

CHAPTER SEVEN

Managing Crises (Lessons from SWAT)

Take control • The importance of rehearsal • Conduct shared-goal exercises • Cultivate maturity and good judgment • Debrief! and institutionalize best practices • Keep them well • Make decisions without second-guessing

> Let's face it, the good guys are in the "reaction business."
> It's the bad guys who initiate the force.
>
> —CRAIG ARNOLD, SWAT COMMANDER

The FBI is very proactive. Its intelligence-led investigations have preempted more threats to society, from all manner of criminal and terrorist enterprises, than we will ever know. But it is not omniscient. Situations arise spontaneously that cry for help—so spontaneously, in fact, that even the perpetrator does not always know his or her actions will precipitate a crisis. When human beings lose control and suddenly start shooting indiscriminately, or take hostages when an armed robbery goes wrong, or barricade themselves in their homes, there is often no warning. At the other end of the threat spectrum are the nonspontaneous assaults on society—the terrorist attacks that, though carefully planned, have evaded the radar. In either case, the FBI may not be omniscient, but it is ready.

If the FBI, with its unparalleled intelligence-gathering network, can be surprised, how can the average company hope to escape the traumatic business challenges that occasionally erupt within and from outside the workplace?

Take Control

What could be a more helpless position than being on the other end of the phone as an electronically disguised voice threatens to kill your child unless demands are met? Anger and outrage would have to be stifled lest the kidnapper, who holds all the cards, is provoked. The horror of the situation is such that we will do anything the voice demands, anything, to regain our loved one. The demands are followed so explicitly that some parents do not call the FBI until days have passed. When the agents arrive on the scene they are in the same predicament as the parents—not knowing the whereabouts or the condition of the child. The FBI may have the electronic gadgetry and the surveillance capability, but the fact remains that the innocent child is under the complete control of the kidnapper.

Even a SWAT team, for all its firepower, would seem to be at the mercy of a hostage taker, since the safety of the hostage is SWAT's primary concern. All demands of the hostage taker are backed by the threat of instant death for the hostage(s), and that threat is reinforced by the rapidly deteriorating mental condition of the hostage taker. And since the FBI agents are, in the words of legendary former SWAT Commander Craig Arnold, "reactive," it might be assumed that by "reacting" to the demands of desperate, armed criminals, the agents are not in the driver's seat. Ostensibly, that is true enough—at least that's what the hostage takers are made to believe. But by utilizing a kind of mental jujitsu, the SWAT team members "react" by taking advantage of the initiatives directed against them. When the bad guys "push," they "pull."

By apparently ceding to the demands of the kidnapper or hostage taker, the FBI negotiators buy a little more time, which allows the rest of their resources to deploy—to seek out the kidnapper or to control the remaining options of the hostage taker. Always mindful of the plight of the innocent and doubtless terrified hostage, the SWAT team is a model of patience. "Our philosophy is to wait it out," explains Craig Arnold, "unless there is obvious harm being done inside to the hostages. The longer the negotiator talks to them, the more likely things will be resolved without shots being fired. If the negotiator doesn't get it done, we'll get it done. But I'd much rather have him get it done," he grins.

Tom Zyckowski, the FBI negotiator at more tense situations than he cares to remember, elaborates. "The negotiator will let the bad guy think he's in control, at least in the building he's holed up in, while tactfully reminding him that outside he's surrounded by SWAT. We offer enticements for concessions, for example food and water in exchange for a hostage. Other enticements might include cigarettes, toiletries, the promise not to turn off heat or AC and electricity, TV news coverage, etc. Loved ones of the bad guy may be briefed and used as negotiators unless there's a reason not to, for example if the cops think the bad guy will kill himself or a hostage in order to punish the relative. As negotiators, we show empathy for the bad guy, downplaying the seriousness of events to date, pointing out his emotions to him, echoing his statements, showing concern for him, his injuries, his family. We don't threaten force; we gain his trust. Every step of the way, the bad guy loses more control of the situation to the negotiator."

The idea of taking control where no control seems attainable is fascinating, and it has definite business applications, because our customers make demands too, and some of them can be fairly outrageous. They demand we meet their "final" price even after we've outbid all competitors for the job. They demand we meet their schedule after waiting until the last minute, thereby depriving us of precious ramp-up time. They demand that we agree to their billing and payment terms. They want us to deliver to sites we hadn't anticipated. They ask that we inventory for them, that we indemnify them, that we extend more credit. And if we hesitate to accept these terms under considerable pressure, the customers tell us they will "find somebody who will."

Confronted with these kinds of demands, we can't (unfortunately) call in an FBI SWAT team, but we can take a lesson from the hostage negotiator and make a frank assessment of the customer's true position as the customer tries to take our profits "hostage."

The customer's relative power over us, upon consideration, may be much more tenuous than it would appear. For one thing, she needs a reliable vendor, and she wouldn't be talking to us if she didn't think us capable. Her choice of credible alternatives is much more limited than she would have us believe as she shakes a handful of competitive bids before us, brandishing apples to oranges. The customer may in fact be desperate in terms of time. After all, she has a customer too, upline, that must be satisfied. She may have heard good things about us from her business pals, or she may have been impressed by our good reputation. And for all of her bluster, she may have already made up her mind to give us the contract!

The customer may well soften her stance and eventually withdraw or amend her demands if we do not come on too strongly. In other words, instead of pushing back, we "pull." While expressing sympathy with her demands, we may yet be able to wrest a measure of control. We can show her how her vision can be brought to reality if she would only partner with us on certain aspects of the project. If she demands a pricing concession, we may agree, provided she pays periodic, advance cash deposits throughout the project. By appealing to her sense of fair play, we may be able to get her to agree to accept direct shipments from the factory for certain materials, relieving us of being the middleman.

One thing is for certain: The customer has withheld from us margins of cost and schedule. We know that because we would too in her position, and in fact we do it all the time with our own suppliers. We also do it in our personal life. If we needed a backyard patio installed by the Fourth of July for a big barbecue bash, would we tell the prospective contractor we needed it by July 3rd? We would instead give ourselves a little slack (margin) and probably tell him the patio must be completed by the 10th of May. If he asks us the amount we have budgeted for the patio, are we going to tell him the truth and give him the exact amount, or will we hold back some margin, perhaps by reducing our actual budget by 25 percent? That contractor, if he is smart, will not directly oppose us by saying the job cannot be done in that time frame with that budget. He will instead get us to surrender, bit by bit, our unrevealed margin.

The Importance of Rehearsal

When an FBI SWAT team arrives on the scene, the special weapons team of local law enforcement has sometimes already established positions. Conversely, an FBI SWAT team may be "spelled" by the local team after tense hours of being poised for action. In either case, the SWAT team takes advantage of that "free time" to rehearse.

Craig Arnold explains: "Whenever we have the opportunity, we'll rehearse the emergency assault. Each guy will go through his plan, like actors rehearsing their roles and their positions on the stage. Hopefully we'll have a blueprint to work off of or a similar building next door to rehearse in. If not, we'll draw the floor plan on the parking lot pavement with chalk and go through our movements again and again."

One might think that after hundreds of hours of the best training in the world, a SWAT team commander might assume his "cast" is so familiar with their roles that rehearsal isn't necessary. In fact, it might appear to the rest of us that there is no time for rehearsal; the crisis is the real thing! Besides, the SWAT team members have already practiced a thousand simulated entries through a thousand doorways during their training. These professionals can accurately envision each step they will soon take. Nevertheless, the elite SWAT team rehearses on "opening night" with the earnestness of actors making their debuts.

"Rehearsals are critical," maintains Los Angeles SWAT Commander Dale Monroe, "because you're improving your chances the more you rehearse. If you have a floor plan, you rehearse the operation so that once you get inside, all you have to worry about are the unknowns. Of course, if you don't have a floor plan, then just about everything is unknown, so you fall back on your training."

Commander Monroe couldn't have put it better. The elimination of unknowns is precisely what rehearsal is all about. Having liberated their conscious minds to focus only on the few remaining unknowns, the SWAT team members are able to walk undistracted into situations that strike us as nightmarish. We've all had frightening dreams of wandering through a disorienting maze of darkened corridors lined with shut doors that conceal some kind of menace. SWAT members are psychologically able to walk down those darkened corridors and kick through the doors in real life, thanks to incomprehensible courage, incessant training, and on-the-spot rehearsals.

One of the most important "unknowns" to eliminate is the question of one's own behavior. Panic is not knowing what to do. Through rehearsal, SWAT members learn what to do on a nearly cellular level, through physical repetition. "If the training is good enough and done frequently enough," explains Commander Monroe, "muscle memory is created, and muscle memory can compensate for a lot. In an emergency you can react through muscle memory no matter how you're feeling, and before you know it the emergency has passed."

The prospect of rehearsal is not particularly welcomed in the business environment for a number of reasons: (a) rehearsals are difficult to organize; (b) the time spent just getting all the "players" together could have been better spent on job-specific responsibilities; (c) *group* rehearsals are unnecessary, since each individual is responsible for (and has committed to) knowing his or her part; (d) some employees, like salespeople, are not yet ready and do not want anyone else to know; and (e) some employees, again like salespeople, want to be spontaneous rather than offer a "canned" presentation to the customer.

When it comes to preparation, many of us live by the "just in time" management philosophy we abided by in college. It is probably safe to say that relatively few of us would begin to cram fully six weeks before a final exam, even though the date loomed on the calendar. There are so many other tests and papers due in the meantime. And besides, it might be counterproductive. Those of us who were accomplished "test takers" grew accustomed to retaining large blocks of information for a minimum amount of time. By cramming the night before an exam, we hoped to remember the answers to the questions just long enough to pass the test and then move on, "just in time," to the next challenge.

Rehearsals are unpopular because they require us to know our part well before the event. We are forced to confront the challenge much sooner than we'd rather. But a good manager will insist on individual and group rehearsals to identify problems well before the actual event. No individual, incidentally, should be allowed to consider a group presentation as a series of individual performances, including his or her own. A customer presentation can be larger or smaller than the sum of its parts, and that desired synergy is created by group rehearsals, which not only help ensure a smooth transition between the participants but enable them to learn enough of their associates' presentation to cover for the others should there be a slipup. Even thoroughly rehearsed SWAT professionals are capable of a misstep in the heat of action. "If one of our guys turns right, instead of left, as rehearsed," confides Craig Arnold, "the guy following him through the door will have the flexibility of mind to compensate, because during rehearsals we get a chance to see the other guys play their roles."

Rehearsals also allow us to help one another perfect our parts in the presentation, so that information is not needlessly (and irritatingly) duplicated in front of the customer. If the participants on the sales team were to prepare separately and simply show up on the big day, there is every chance that the transition from segment to segment would be awkward. Many of us have had the disconcerting experience of waiting "our turn" to participate in a group presentation only to hear our predecessor address the topic we have prepared. After all, they're nervous too and sometimes grab at sentences like a drowning man at straws. The more a major presentation is rehearsed, the less likely it is to fail to persuade the customer. A group presentation is, after all, a miniportrait of the company being represented. If the customer sees a well-coordinated display of product knowledge, with seamless handoffs from one presenter to another, the customer will assume the company's other handoffs—from sales to installation to service—are equally seamless.

Conduct Shared-Goal Exercises

A desperate bank robber with his back to the wall, surrounded by police cars and FBI SWAT, is apt to be surprised by his first point of contact with law enforcement. Instead of a rough command to "come out with your hands up!" he may hear a calm, and calming, voice over the "throw phone" he has just received. The voice will introduce himself or herself as a member of the FBI's crisis negotiation unit and then ask for *his* name. "We can't talk," the hostage negotiator will say quite reasonably, "without knowing each other's names, can we? Are you okay? Are you hurt?" And thus begins the destressing of a volatile situation.

The FBI has demonstrated time after time its eagerness to end a potentially violent standoff peacefully.

In March 2003, a distraught farmer with a permit to demonstrate near the White House suddenly declared over his bullhorn that the tractor he was driving was filled with explosives. A forty-eight-hour standoff ensued. Even though the farmer could have been "taken out" by any number of FBI and White House police snipers in an instant, the voice of a female negotiator could be heard pleading, "Come on, Dwight, you said you were coming out. You gave me your word. Come out now." To the relief of everyone, the farmer surrendered. There were no explosives. He had just snapped.

In 2001, two prison escapees were discovered in a Colorado RV park. Completely surrounded by local police and FBI agents, the convicts faced a stark choice: Return to lifelong jail sentences under unbearable conditions, or go out in a blaze of glory. In discussions with the hostage negotiator, they bitterly denounced the Texas prison system, from which they had escaped, vowing never to return. "I didn't know it was that bad," responded the negotiator. "You've got a story to tell. The whole world should hear about this." The desperadoes, who saw a third alternative—being "whistle-blowers" of a sort—finally surrendered. During the standoff, dozens of assault weapons had been pointed at the thin aluminum walls of the RV. The FBI was in a position of unassailable power, yet it chose to try every means possible to end the crisis without firing a shot.

Sometimes, "the means" are so creative as to border on the unbelievable. In 1996, the eighty-one-day siege of the antigovernment separatist group calling itself the Freemen ended peacefully after the FBI chauffeured its ringleader to jail so he could speak with his imprisoned uncle, and then *back again* to his Montana compound, where he persuaded his followers to surrender!

In a crisis situation, it is interesting that the hostage negotiator is an FBI agent and not, for example, a psychiatrist recruited from the medical community or a psychological counselor from academia. That possibility is not quite as far-fetched as it first appears. Hollywood depictions of hostage negotiators always seem to put them in an antagonistic relationship with the SWAT commander, as if a hostage negotiation were a kind of arbitration between the FBI and the perpetrator or a conflict resolution requiring an impartial third party. That the hostage negotiator trains with the rest of the SWAT team is even more interesting. After all, he or she is trying to relieve them from having to go to work at all.

Although they share the ultimate goal of a nonviolent solution to the crisis, the job specialties of the hostage negotiator and the SWAT members are contrasting. One wants to defuse the situation; the other is poised to rush in.

Why would the FBI want the *antithesis* to train with the *thesis?* The question may be best answered by asking instead, What would it be like if the two elements trained separately? That is, what if they trained like the business community trains?

Well, the hostage negotiator would spend his or her time studying crisis resolution, while the SWAT team would perfect the coordinated assault techniques required if resolution proved to be impossible. The negotiator would become expert in the art of persuasion, the SWAT member in the application of physical force. One would train to open the door, the other to kick it down. Both, of course, would have separate career paths and success metrics to meet. When they'd meet on site, each would recognize that the success of one implied the failure of the other. They would set about their tasks as adversaries instead of partners. What would be lost in this fanciful and unproductive working relationship is the plight of the unfortunate hostage, whose safety should be of paramount concern to both. Fortunately for the poor hostage, there is no conflict of goals between the negotiator and the rest of SWAT. "They have to know what we do; we have to know what they do," explains Craig Arnold. "It's a partnership. The Hollywood movies that portray the SWAT team leader as impatient to get in there and shoot the place up are total nonsense. I'd much rather have the hostages—and even the hostage taker—walk out alive because of the success of the negotiator."

Sharing a common goal (in this case, the release of the unharmed hostage) makes the SWAT partnership work. Training together helps each party appreciate the other's contribution to that goal. If only more organizations followed this model!

It seems that in many companies, the goal is to protect and perpetuate the agenda of each department rather than to serve a satisfied customer. It's not at all unusual for the various departments in an organization to quietly disparage one another. Salespeople believe R&D unnecessarily delays a product's release by obsessive tinkering. Installation managers scratch their heads at the job site and wonder if the salesperson ever even glanced at a blueprint, while customer service technicians resent being put in the position of dealing with a customer who has been promised the moon by the salesperson. Manufacturing wants to keep things simple, while quality control wants to implement Six Sigma. The controller wants to reduce the training budget, while the training department points out the costs of having to correct the mistakes in the field caused by insufficient training. What gets lost here is the desire on the part of the customer to experience a confirmation of its buying decision every step of the way—from the conception, to the sale, to the installation, to the proper functioning of the purchased equipment, to the scheduled maintenance.

While it would be unrealistic to expect each department's representative to sit in on the training of his or her counterpart for any length of time, it is certainly feasible to have shared-goal exercises once or twice a year that involve everyone concerned. It could all begin with a simulated RFP (request for proposal) that delineates the customer's wishes in terms of product performance expectations, production standards, installation requirements, maintenance agreements, etc.—complete with blueprints, specification books, and sample contract. The desired end point would be a satisfied customer during every phase of the journey, not the satisfaction of departmental goals. In fact, as the training exercise develops, it may become clear that one department will have to sacrifice meeting one of its own success metrics in order for the company to achieve the ultimate goal. The sales department may have to donate some of its required margin so that customer service can meet the maintenance contract cost requirements. Manufacturing may need to raise its overhead and thereby fail to meet an important operations metric, in order for sales to guarantee the scheduled rollout desired by the customer.

Instead of doing things the old way—with each department signing off on its "completed" portion of the scope of work, then passing it on to the next department—the separate sectors are forced to approach the project as a unified company. By huddling over the planning table together, the various department members will develop a deeper understanding and appreciation of each other's concerns and responsibilities. Meanwhile, the facilitator, playing the role of the customer, floats through the room from one discussion to another, serving as a reminder of the ultimate goal.

The socialization aspect of a significant shared-goal exercise is not to be underestimated. The benefits of disparate departmental members being compelled to consult, consort, and collaborate with one another are manifest. It is likely that a number of misconceptions and stereotypes will be shattered through familiarization. Customer service reps may discover that their counterparts in sales are serious professionals, not carefree gladhanders. The quality control manager may find many values in common with the "full speed ahead" production manager. Friendships will be struck, and people will learn whom to go to in the future for expert advice. A sense of obligation will develop—not to a department but to a new friend, whose interests will now be considered rather than dismissed. It's easy for departments to have adversarial relationships, but much more difficult for human beings on a first-name basis. Knowledge will be shared as tips are passed along from one department to another. It may be of interest to a salesperson, for example, that the product she is selling is much more easily serviced in the field than the offerings of her competitor—this she learns from a customer service tech who used to work for the competitor. Similarly, the installation department may be grateful to learn from manufacturing that a simple on-site product modification can save hours of fitting and adjusting.

Shared-goal training, emphasized through customer satisfaction exercises, has a pollinating effect throughout an organization. Departmental fiefdoms cannot sustain themselves in a blooming corporate culture. The FBI has known this for generations. Despite budget cuts and despite the universal trend toward increasing specialization, it has found a way to train broadly and holistically. Today's lean and mean organization would do well to invest in this kind of training doctrine.

Cultivate Maturity and Good Judgment

Of all the traits one might think a SWAT commander looks for in his teammates—such as mental alertness, courage, physical endurance—the highest valued of all are maturity and good judgment. "Everybody in law enforcement has to have courage," explains Dale Monroe. "Look at what a police officer does when he or she approaches a blacked-out car pulled over in the middle of the night. You can't do that if you don't have courage. But first and foremost, the hostage rescue team and SWAT assess someone's judgment."

Craig Arnold puts it this way: "We can teach somebody to shoot. We can train them to be physically fit. But if a person isn't mature we can't make him mature. If he doesn't have good judgment, we can't wave a magic wand and give it to him. So we look for these attributes up front."

One can certainly understand why maturity and good judgment would be critical in a hair-trigger hostage situation, in which an impetuous move or an overreaction could quite easily cause the death of innocent citizens and fellow SWAT or hostage rescue team members. And while the best training in the world can further cultivate these traits, it must be admitted the FBI has an advantage over most organizations in this respect: The average age of Academy trainees is thirty years. Its agents, furthermore, are already accomplished professionals, degreed, and highly motivated. The SWAT commanders may have to look for maturity and judgment, but they don't have to look far.

In the business world, where the screening process and the probationary periods are not nearly as rigorous as in the FBI, such qualities cannot be taken for granted. Indeed, immaturity and poor judgment are frequently the cause of scandals at the highest levels of the organization. If the CEOs end up on the front pages of the newspaper, or in prison, it can be assumed that their fatal character flaws persist in middle management and in the rank and file. After all, that's where they came from on their long climb up the corporate ladder.

There is another reason why companies sometimes get into trouble: They don't want maturity for certain job descriptions because a mature applicant would recognize the ludicrousness of the offer. Certain entry-level jobs in sales that require nonstop door-to-door cold calling—sometimes euphemistically referred to as "farmer" or "hunter" positions—call for youthful energy and naiveté. A more mature sales applicant, who would know the chances of making a sale compared to the energy expended, would say, "Are you kidding?" When trying to fill job positions that have a high burnout rate (telemarketing, fast-food sales, auto sales, etc.), management does not look for maturity except in the case of elderly part-time work, and then it interprets "maturity" as "desperation." On the contrary, only an ingenue will be susceptible to the glowing vision created by the telemarketing recruiter, who knows full well the new hire will not last, statistically, more than a few months. The problem is that these younger, less mature employees are often on the front lines of customer service. They are, in fact, the first point of contact for the customer and are thereby in a position to do as much harm as good.

A harried or rude receptionist, or a service technician who loses his temper in front of a customer, or a fast-food counter person who chats with his or her friends while simultaneously ignoring legitimate customers in line, can cause problems out of all proportion to their low wages. In the ranks of management, where people should know better, immature behavior can result in million-dollar sexual harassment lawsuits against the company—not against the offender, who has long since gone. And poor judgment in the upper reaches of senior management can lead to subsequent cover-ups that become inextricable and ultimately scandalous.

How, then, can a company cultivate maturity and sound judgment throughout the organization?

A conscientious mentoring program is a good start, especially for entry-level employees who are in front of the customer. When a young person's role model is a "company man" or a "company woman"—as opposed to a cynical, fast-talking, and opportunistic associate—the chances are his attempts to emulate will be more in line with the best interests of the company. When a mentor not only teaches by example but shows great interest in the employee's professional development, discussing over quarterly lunches his progress with career development courses and company-subsidized continuing education, the self-esteem of the employee soars. He will want to demonstrate he's worth the investment. When an entry-level employee feels as if he is on a career path and not just paying the rent, it will matter less that the first step on that career path is so ignominious. A person who considers himself a future leader will try to act like one regardless of his current position, which is a stepping-stone rather than a dead end.

The mentor is a philosopher, not a trainer. And the newcomer in all probability needs a philosopher. The company must not assume that the newly hired employee has been inculcated by the popular culture with the desired work ethic and organizational values.

In fact, it is likely just the opposite has happened, well before he has been hired. Business gurus on television and in the glossy magazines have advised the newcomer to develop, in her own economic self-defense, a free-agent mentality. She has been told that "company men" are relics from the past, unimaginative plodders afraid to leave their comfort zone, while the up-and-coming top performer has an "exit strategy" and jumps from organization to organization, enhancing her résumé with every higher leap. Once the newcomer joins the corporation and once she graduates from "basic training," she is susceptible to even more counterproductive messages from her own associates. If she is in sales, her new teammates show her the "street-smart" way to get things done. She will be told in so many words that the company is her adversary: "Management will impose a salary cap with unrealistic bonus-related goals. They will cut your territory in half next year if you exceed your quota this year. They will transfer you into an uncharted market, where you'll have to start all over again."

These (hopefully inaccurate) messages must be countered by an aggressive mentoring program if a company wishes its interests to remain in the forefront of the employee's consciousness—and conscience. A mentor, chosen for his or her dedication to the values of the corporation rather than solely for a personal record of achievement, is the warm personification of the company. He or she is living proof that a dignified career is possible within the organization and that decency is rewarded with lots of business and job security. A mentor is also a non-competing role model; there is no question of a personal agenda. A good mentor is a kind of angel, a transition figure who guides the freshly anointed into the new corporate life and exists in memory as a personal example of the rewards possible when the interests of the company are put ahead of quick ambition. A mentor is also the person to go to when the new hire is ethically conflicted and unsure of which path to take.

Maturity and judgment can also be developed on the job by placing one's people in leadership positions as often as possible—as a team leader, or in charge of a special project, or as the coordinator of the company picnic, or as the facilitator of a charity car wash. Placing an employee in any leadership position, no matter how menial, is better than allowing him to think in terms only of himself. In addition to giving assignments of responsibility in which subordinates will look to him for leadership, it would be wise to expose the young employee to critical-thinking sessions involving issues that are way above his pay grade. He could be invited, for example, to occasionally sit in during management meetings as an observer, or to go on "ride alongs" with a manager once a quarter. Overtures like these cost the company nothing, yet they make a positive impression on the young employee whose eyes have been opened to strategic thinking and to the possible long-term consequences of thoughtless actions.

Another cost-effective way to cultivate maturity is to appoint a company historian, not as a collector of scrapbook memorabilia but as a teacher and philosopher who frequently gives presentations to both the rank and file and management. When employees begin to look at their company from a biographical perspective, their own role in the company narrative becomes conspicuous.

Debrief! and Institutionalize Best Practices

A SWAT standoff can take hours, days, and—in some of the more famous stalemates with boarded-up cults—months. A long shift "on point" puts a tremendous mental and physical strain on the entire team, as each member remains poised to move in at a moment's notice. Often the only physical relief from the sustained nervous tension comes when the command is given to bust through the door, which of course brings its own dangers. At the end of an operation, the SWAT team may be exhausted. One might think the team members would finally be allowed to go home, crawl into bed, and get some sleep before beginning their twelve-hour "day jobs" as street agents. But that isn't quite the case.

"I don't care how tired we are," explains Craig Arnold, "we'll go back to the office, sit around a table, still dressed in our jumpsuits, and talk about what we did right, what we did wrong, and how to make it better next time."

There are a few compelling reasons for an immediate after-action review. First and foremost is the possibility of forgetting important details if the debriefing is postponed. Tom Zyckowski explains: "You've got to do this when the memory is fresh. No matter how tired you are, the memory will be better before you sleep, not after." Second, the team leader wants to recapture the event in total, for the benefit of every team member. "You've got to remember," elaborates Craig Arnold, "some of the guys on the team, depending on their positions, might not have seen all the action. By sitting in on the debriefing, the whole picture will come clear to them." And, third, the lessons learned must be not only incorporated into team strategy for future events, they must be passed on to the entire organization so that a SWAT team on the other side of the country can benefit from the mistakes made and by the best practices.

The business community has much to learn from the emphasis the FBI places on debriefings.

After-action reviews in the business world, to the degree to which they happen at all, are generally reserved for initiatives that went wrong, not for the ones that went right. Successes are celebrated immediately and are not subjected to serious debriefings. If there were mistakes made, they are airily dismissed by jubilant executives who don't want to dwell on negatives or look a gift horse in the mouth. But successful individual and team efforts should be put under even more scrutiny than unsuccessful attempts because the techniques that proved efficacious should be identified, thoroughly understood, and institutionalized into corporate policy for the next challenge. And even if luck had a great deal to do with the final outcome, it may be possible to replay the events and discover what management approaches *could* have led to the same happy conclusion. But often, none of this seems necessary to management in the flush of victory.

When does management want to "get to the bottom" of an individual or team initiative? Only when it has failed. Managers who often had nothing to do with the venture will convene a postmortem and search—not for the mistake, but for the person who made the mistake. The business equivalent of a "debriefing" is a fault-finding session, the purpose of which is to assign blame ("responsibility"). In this kind of inquisitorial setting, the uncomfortable team members being interrogated are not apt to be open with their thoughts. Most of their mental energy will be spent coming up with clever, defensive answers. Since nobody is thinking far beyond his or her next paycheck at this point, there will be no attempt to find the true cause of the failed effort for the benefit of all the other employees who are currently engaged in similar missions. The organization is not likely to learn from the mistakes that were made, because the mistakes, per se, are not studied.

It is a much different atmosphere in a SWAT debriefing, where even exhausted team members are thinking of how the next SWAT action might benefit from the one just completed. Craig Arnold had little problem eliciting honest feedback. "I would tell them, 'Guys, we've got to be candid. We're SWAT brothers, we love each other, but we've got to be open. If someone screwed up, let's learn from our mistakes so nothing bad happens to us next time. Be critical of yourself. If you made a mistake tell us about it. Or if you did something good, or saw someone else do something good, tell us about that too.'"

The lessons learned are then put into writing. "Either the SWAT commander or one of his team leaders," continues Tom Zyckowski, "will take notes and write a report that spells out exactly what happened during the course of the incident. That report follows an operations order which is done *before* the action, which describes what the mission will be, how people are assigned, where the nearest hospitals are, what communication channels will be used, etc. There is always a before and after report. The after report gets reviewed by, among others, the SWAT unit at headquarters in Washington, D.C., and if they feel there are valuable lessons to be learned, a training memo will be sent out to all SWAT teams in the field and will eventually get immortalized in the SWAT training manual or the crisis negotiation manual."

"We also have annual SWAT team leader conferences," Craig Arnold concludes, "in which we share best practices. We'll share our mistakes too, so other SWAT teams can learn. It's all very open and honest. No egos get in the way, because this is a brotherhood."

No businessperson would argue that something new is

learned on every project, but how many have actually witnessed the mechanism by which this newfound knowledge is incorporated into company policy? There are companies that make the effort to share success stories from their various branches, but even with a "spotlight on success" newsletter there is no guarantee that it is actually read by those who need the information the most. It is human nature to look upon our challenges as unprecedented. A perfectly natural egotism leads us to believe that there is no one quite like ourselves and certainly no one like our customer. We believe the set of circumstances we find ourselves in is unique and requires a unique solution. We even consider our moment in time, in which there is a technical renaissance, to be completely without parallel in history. And it takes a certain maturity to realize that we are not particularly special nor are the principles of our business challenges unprecedented.

But even if success tips are incorporated into the company manual, corporate policy is often held in contempt by the employees, who want to be recognized for "thinking outside the box" and who prefer "street-smart" solutions to the excessively protective ways of the patriarchs and the matriarchs of the company, who hang in gilded frames on the wall like ancestors from an irrelevant age. There are a great many salespeople, for example, who consider the company manual to be a hindrance, an obstacle to success, not a virtual coach that will help them succeed off the experiences of others who have been in similar situations.

It is impossible to know how much time and energy is wasted reinventing the wheel, but it is safe to say that the larger the organization the more important it is to share and institutionalize best practices. Employees at one branch have counterparts at other branches who have identical responsibilities and who face similar challenges. What works for one may very well work for another. But for a number of reasons, managers seem to have a tough time getting employees to share their experiences, and the managers are not blameless themselves.

We have all heard the expression, voiced with admiration and perhaps tinged with envy, "I don't know how he does it!" The person referred to may be quite willing to let his admirers continue to wonder, as it adds to his mystique. But from the company's perspective, stated ignorance of a top performer's "secrets to success" should be a signal of poor management. There should be no question of "how he does it." The company should know exactly how he does it, down to the very last detail, not only to share his technique and enable others to duplicate his success, but to render the successful employee "replaceable" should he ever leave the company. And, of course, this is where the tension exists.

Most high performers are quite willing to share—indeed, to *announce*—their successes, but usually in broad strokes. When pressed for details they may be less forthcoming. Assuming that he has something to share and that his triumph was not pure luck, the top performer is constrained by self-interest. It is a fact of life that to share is to diminish one's personal value to the company. That the company gains through the gift of sharing means little to a free-agent mentality. He wants to play his cards close to the vest to keep his managers guessing. The less they know "how he does it," the more they will value him.

Another consideration is personal ambition. If a top performer is doing something well, why should he share with an associate who is also a rival? Why should he qualify others for the promotion he himself covets? He learned his particular skills the hard way, so why present those hard-won lessons to a competitor on a silver platter? And if sharing must be done, why not do it when he can get maximum credit, such as at the annual awards dinner, at the podium in front of the assembly, where he can be praised for not only developing a successful technique but for unselfishly sharing it with his associates!

It's different in the FBI. The mutually experienced sense of mission throughout the workforce makes the communication of best practices a no-brainer. It saves lives. But in a business setting, lives are not at stake, only contracts, and one's primary responsibility is to oneself, not to the organization.

If management is to communicate and perpetuate best practices throughout the organization, it will sometimes have to extract the information. Top performers must be engaged in the communication process and occasionally pinned down, perhaps over lunch with a senior executive who asks the necessary probing questions. They could also be given an assignment to share, perhaps to give a "war stories" presentation before the entire department. These solicited techniques can then be added to an accessible library of shared best practices for the benefit of their counterparts.

Having gained and indexed the secrets to success, management must then convince its employees that there is an incredible resource available to them that will save time, energy, and anxiety. But chances are, management will find that it is just as difficult to get its people to make use of its treasure trove of successful techniques as it was to compile it in the first place.

Given the breathtaking pace of technological development, many employees may be apt to dismiss the dusty old company manual as irrelevant to the "unprecedented" challenges faced today. And given the emphasis of "thinking outside the box," other people's achievements are not to be emulated, but rendered obsolete by a new, creative approach that will make one's reputation within the organization. So the best practices that have been so carefully transcribed by management may very well be ignored.

Management cannot allow proven techniques to be cob-webbed. They must be promoted through open discussion with the workforce. If the employees won't go to the company manual, the manual must be brought to them, perhaps within the framework of interactive sessions in which the challenge (as it once appeared to the top performer) is presented to the audience and possible solutions are solicited. After acknowledging these suggestions (an interesting and productive exercise in itself!), the best practice being celebrated can be introduced and explored in depth. *Why* did the technique work, and will it work in all situations? Could it have been even more effective if slightly modified? If one had to do it over again, could it be improved?

Equally provocative, and in its own way perhaps even more enlightening, would be group analyses of approaches that didn't work. It goes without saying that a tremendous amount of trust would be required for an employee to be forthcoming with his or her failures, but a charismatic manager can bring this about. Indeed, the right manager can make the experience positively cathartic. There is great relief in confession, not only for the individual concerned, but for the group, which sees the employee treated fairly and compassionately. They can see that it won't be so bad when their turns come. "Sharing sessions" can be so entertaining and so instructive that the powerful techniques presented will likely be remembered, if not in detail then as a reference point to be accessed when confronted with a similar challenge.

Employees don't make use of best practices because they are either unaware of them or do not appreciate their relevancy. Both conditions are failures of management.

Without a conscious effort on the part of management to perpetuate the experiences of the few into helpful, perhaps project-saving, suggestions for the many, the organization will suffer unnecessary hits to the bottom line. Every manager has a fiduciary duty to prepare the organization for the next challenge presented by the marketplace. If a self-corrective spirit can be created and sustained even in moments of defeat, our employees will be positively eager to find fault in their own actions and less likely to make the same mistake twice. The debriefing sessions for projects, won or lost, will not be dreaded. And no project, including the "flawless" ones, will be considered complete until the after-action review.

Keep Them Well

One of the greatest threats to "mission readiness" in the workplace has nothing to do with the serious leadership challenges so many books have been written about. Yet it is insidious, counterproductive, and spreads through departments faster than a rumor, affecting morale to the point where employees will be seen reaching for tissues.

It is the common cold.

An often overlooked management responsibility is the *physical* well-being of one's people. But most of us would not consider the common cold a management issue. Unless we happen to be SWAT commanders.

Given the responsibilities of SWAT and the state of readiness that must be maintained twenty-four/seven, the health of its members cannot be taken for granted. It would be a serious thing indeed if half the team were to be incapacitated with stomach flu, or if a sniper "on point" developed a chronic cough, or if a team member stealthily creeping through a window as part of a surprise assault sneezed. To avoid these kinds of situations, the tough-as-nails SWAT commander has to be a bit of a mother hen.

"Before taking some of my guys to Nairobi, Kenya, in 1998 after the embassy bombing," reveals Craig Arnold, "I made sure everyone got their battery of shots before departure. I also ensured that they took their malaria pills while deployed and that we always ate together and stayed together as a team wherever we went."

Sometimes Craig would even take a doctor along.

"We developed a strong relationship with an emergency room doctor in Kansas City. He was an FBI contractor, with FBI credentials, who deployed with us on numerous occasions. On our forty-day mission at the Winter Olympics, he was with us in Salt Lake City. Not long after we arrived, several guys developed flu symptoms, with one operator down hard in bed. Our doctor—armed with some FBI Kansas City Olympic pins, patches, and hats—went to the clinic in Olympic Village that treated the athletes and was able to obtain some serious antibiotics. Almost overnight our guys felt better. Without the doctor and his prompt care, the entire team may have been down with the flu, our ability to accomplish our mission seriously degraded."

A manager in the normal workplace would not consider it her responsibility to make sure everyone in the department got a flu shot, took his or her vitamins, and lived a healthy lifestyle in general. She would think it none of her business, and if the manager presumed to intrude on the private lifestyles of her people, *they* would think it none of her business. But is that really true? The workplace performance levels of her people *are* matters of business and are dependent on the health of the individuals. If a team member exhibits poor health habits, manifested in frequent sick days, a manager has every right to be concerned. But does she have the right to intervene?

The presumption that management has a vested interest in the health habits of its employees has already been established—through the ubiquitous random drug test. Most employees accept with equanimity that they must occasionally donate bodily fluids into a lab specimen cup, even though there has been nothing in their behavior to suggest drug use. They have also accepted the nonsmoking workplace mandate. So there is precedent. Managers should not feel as if they have to passively watch the health of their employees deteriorate to the point where performance falters, at which point they can "officially" step in. The proactive manager is entitled to step in well before the employee's poor health habits cost his or her department.

It all begins with personal example. A manager who radiates physical well-being can serve as a role model for those who truly dislike their own addictions—alcohol, tobacco, overeating, etc.—and who are looking for a leader to help them change. And there is a lot a charismatic manager can do. He or she can start up evening or morning jogging (or walking) clubs and let it be known that anyone who wants to join in the fun will be welcome. Aside from the obvious health benefits, these activities will give both manager and team members a chance to get to know one another better, in a playful setting. The manager can sponsor weekly potluck lunches with an accent on nutrition. Recipe sharing can be encouraged, with little prizes awarded for the tastiest healthful dishes. Voluntary weight loss contests can be held, or, if that might make some employees uncomfortable, the manager can announce his or her own quest to lose weight and "weigh in" periodically in front of the department, with much comic fanfare.

If an individual chronically drags his or her feet on Monday after a wild weekend, the manager can give that person assignments *due* on Monday morning, thus putting a crimp in the weekend lifestyle. In any case, such an individual should be counseled. And sometimes a simple statement like "I'm counting on you, because you are critical to the functioning of this team" is enough to create a sense of obligation to arrive on Mondays chipper and alert.

The manager has to make it clear to all concerned that absenteeism costs the company money, and anything that detracts from a profitable operation has a direct bearing on the company's ability to grant raises and to keep jobs secure. To that end, a chart can be posted showing a running total of the department's days in a row without illness, just like the one in the warehouse that counts the consecutive days without an accident. Quarterly "iron man" and "iron woman" awards for full attendance can be given out. The manager can update his or her personnel with healthful lifestyle tips from various media sources. "*Stay* Well" cards can be given out periodically, stressing, in a humorous way, the importance of physical well-being to performance on the job and to the health of the organization as a whole. Progressive companies, recognizing this, supplement health club membership fees for the employee and sponsor walkathons, 10K runs, and even health fairs.

The manager cannot rely, however, on the company's support. Her people may work for the organization, but they report to her and spend the day in a working environment reflective of her management style. Perhaps the most important stimulus to departmental health is an enjoyable working environment. If "going to work" is a drudge, employees will take advantage of their allotted sick days, because they are "sick" of work. And this is where a good manager can have an impact.

According to popular culture, we're not supposed to "live for" our jobs. Instead, our jobs are a means to an end; work is a necessary evil. We've all seen the bumper sticker that expresses the popular sentiment, "The worst day fishing beats the best day working." And, perhaps, while stuck in the bumper-to-bumper commute to and from work, we have nodded our weary heads in agreement. But is it really true? Do we dislike our jobs so much that our best day at work could be topped so easily? Is our worst day fishing (or golfing, sailing, fill in the blank) really better than the highlights of our career, like our presentation to management that was so well received, the handshake from a customer who considered our product a godsend, or the solution we came up with to an age-old company problem?

Isn't it just possible that our work has provided us with not only our daily bread but with many valuable life experiences and friendships as well? And, if we're honest with ourselves, hasn't our job in many ways brought out the best in us by making us more cheerful and sociable (and better groomed) than we might be if left to our own devices, by keeping us earnest in our efforts to improve ourselves and to serve others, and by giving us the structure we require for a productive life? The sentiment expressed by the fisherman's bumper sticker is likely true only if we have very limited opportunities to fish (or golf, sail, etc.). It is distressingly untrue for many retirees who can fish whenever they like for as long as they like and who, quite frankly, have had enough fishing to last the rest of their lives!

A good manager can create a working environment that his or her people will feel deprived of if they take an unjustified "sick" day. They won't want to miss the synergy, camaraderie, and good cheer. Furthermore, they won't want to let their manager down—not for fear of retribution, but out of gratitude for the dynamic and exciting workplace he or she has created.

Make Decisions Without Second-Guessing

Making the correct decision in a life-or-death situation can be an agonizing burden on the FBI supervisor in charge, because there are always a number of viable alternatives and the wrong choice could mean the death of an innocent captive. Should the agents risk blowing a kidnap case, for example, by arresting the person picking up "the drop," when that person may only be an unwitting pawn of the mastermind? Do they apprehend the man making the call at the pay phone, when he could be under the gaze of the binoculars? Should this car, or that car, be followed, when "both" is not an option? Should SWAT bust through the door when the hostage taker suddenly refuses to answer the FBI negotiator—when he may be coming to his senses? Dozens of literal life-or-death decisions may confront the agent during the course of a kidnap investigation or in the midst of a critical hostage situation, under conditions when there is no time for reflection.

When *is* there time for reflection? Months, years later, these decisions can return in dreams, or in quiet moments, to haunt an introspective conscience. This kind of second-guessing is frequently depicted in our favorite suspense films: The FBI agent, drinking alone in the wee hours of a sleepless night, stares into the fireplace and questions for the millionth time a fateful decision once made under crisis conditions. Movie scenes like these may seem melodramatic, but the kernel of truth is undeniable.

The consequences of poor decision making during a crisis can plague an honest conscience.

When asked whether he ever now second-guesses the decisions he made during his twenty-seven years with the Bureau as a kidnap case specialist and as a SWAT commander, retired agent Doug Kane answers with untroubled eyes, "I've never second-guessed myself."

"Neither have I," agrees his longtime partner, retired agent Mark Llewellyn. Noticing my incredulity, he adds, "Not once." Together, the two agents have handled dozens of life-or-death crisis situations.

"The secret to decision making during an emergency," explains Doug, "is to always do what is best for the victim. You don't think about catching the bad guys, or retrieving the money, or what this case might mean for your career. You simply pretend that victim is your own son or daughter and you do what's best for their well-being. If you follow that guideline, how can you second-guess yourself?"

Is it really that simple? If we always "put the customer first" in all of our business dealings, especially during a crisis, will we be spared the self-recrimination that so often follows a busted deal or a lost customer?

From the beginning of time, the customer and the provider of goods and services have had conflicting aims in that both want to profit at the other's expense. The provider must look out for its own interests, surely, but its interests are best served by a prospering customer able to afford its services. Conversely, the customer cannot flourish unless its provider(s) flourish.

It has often been noted that the Chinese word-character for "crisis" contains the symbol for "opportunity." The opportunities presented by a business crisis, however, can be self-serving.

Sellers can exploit material shortages by gouging their customers, just as buyers can take advantage of a material surplus. Those of us who serve others (and that's all of us) would be wise to keep Doug Kane's practical advice in mind. Doing what is best for the customer—*especially* during crisis situations, which are rife with "opportunities" for price gouging, unnecessary change orders, inflated customer contracts, etc.—is, in the long run, in our own best interests as well. In this positive sense, every crisis *is* an opportunity . . . to serve the customer. If we take advantage of a situation to further our own interests, the truth will out, and there will be a loss of trust. While our competitor helps the customer with its future needs, we will be left to ponder our fateful decisions.

CHAPTER EIGHT

Managing the Future

Reach out to the next generation • Hire well • Make the
training relevant to future challenges • Cultivate flexibility
of mind • The problem with success

> We had to ask ourselves, "What kind of workforce
> do we need 10 years from now?"
>
> —ROB GRANT, SAC CHICAGO OFFICE

Some of the ways the FBI manages the future have nothing to
do with clandestine intelligence gathering or shaping the global
battlefield to its advantage (areas in which the average company
cannot easily emulate the FBI) and have much more to do with
preparing the organization for whatever comes. Some of these
practices can be of great use to companies in any industry, no
matter what lies ahead.

The Bureau's outreach to the next generation of employees
is unique and worthy of study. Its robust hiring practices greatly
increase the likelihood that equally dedicated personnel will re-

place the warhorses retiring today. Its insistence that training be relevant to the challenges of the future has paid off countless times for the agents "on the street." Discouraging plan worship, the Bureau develops the ability to quickly adapt when anticipated events go awry, an ability that distinguishes the top performer in every organization. And, to its credit, the Bureau recognizes the unintended consequences of success and deals with them forthrightly.

Reach Out to the Next Generation

Talking to an FBI agent is no different from conversing with most other professionals in corporate America, which is not surprising considering that so many of them have law, business management, or accounting degrees. The agents I've interviewed have for the most part reminded me of the managers, executives, and, in some cases, the CEOs I've met and interviewed over the years. They are equally calm, collected, focused, and serious.

Except when you ask them, "Why did you want to be an FBI agent?"

Then there is a fleeting look of adolescent zeal that passes over the face. It's just there for an instant, but the most experienced agent suddenly seems young again. And the answer is invariably, "I've wanted to be an FBI agent ever since I was a kid."

In the case of Special Agent Mary Hogan, she had to wait until the FBI was ready for *her*. "I actually wrote J. Edgar Hoover when I was fourteen," she laughs. "But back in those days, I was told I couldn't be an agent, although I could be in a support function. Nine years later, I saw an ad in the paper stating that 'the FBI was accepting female applicants' and my childhood dream came true."

Not many organizations—or industries, for that matter—are populated with employees who have dreamt about working for them since childhood. One is not likely to hear statements like, "I've wanted to work for Procter & Gamble ever since I was a kid" (or General Electric, International Paper, DuPont, etc.). Obviously there is something about the FBI that has fired the imaginations of generations of boys and girls.

Why would a child want to be an FBI agent? The inspirational sources would, of course, change over the years as newspaper accounts of G-men shooting it out with the likes of John Dillinger evolved into World War II–era films in which even the cleverest of Nazi spies were no match for vigilant FBI agents. The cold war followed, with its own spy sagas popularized in novels and on film. Some of the most popular television series documented the FBI's triumph over the Mob. Whatever the story line, the common, recurring theme of the nation's best pitted against humanity's worst made such an impression on the youth of America that even those who "grew out of it" continue to harbor a warm respect for the FBI, as indicated by the awe of jury members whenever an FBI agent takes the stand to testify for the prosecution.

The fires of adolescence never quite die out (for better or for worse). Even the most cynical adult reserves a tender smile for the idealistic notions of his or her youth. One's first love, for example, lives on in memory untarnished by the passage of time. Old girlfriends or boyfriends, never seen again, are granted by hindsight a kind of sainthood. Our early aspirations, which all had something to do with saving the world, are remembered with equal fondness because of their purity, having been spawned before the reality of having to make a living kicked in. It is difficult for many of us to imagine working as an adult in the profession we idolized as a child. But a great many FBI agents have in terms of their career choice married their high school sweethearts. And even if that "sweetheart" hasn't always quite lived up to the unreasonably high expectations of youth, the original fire continues to warm the heart.

Which brings us to the question, "How many kids want to work at *your* company when they grow up?"

It may seem unfair to compare an organization like the FBI, with its widely recognized mystique, to the less dramatically challenged business entity. But on second thought, there are a great many companies that lead adventurous business lives as they build skyscrapers in Dubai, or discover therapies to treat debilitating diseases, or develop software capability that seems to border on benevolent witchcraft. In fact, most of the miracles of our time have been performed by businesses.

The FBI has the advantage—some might say disadvantage—of being the subject of frequent news reports, suspenseful novels, and blockbuster movies, so naturally its exploits, real and embellished, reach a much larger audience. So let's reduce the scope of the question to make it fair: "How many of your employee's kids dream of working at your company when they grow up?"

The answer would depend, of course, on the tenor of the table talk at dinner as mom and dad discuss their respective workdays. But it would also depend on the degree to which the company "marketed" itself to the families of the employees. Does the CEO, for example, host a family day during which all are invited into the facility to see the kinds of projects mom and dad are working on? Are the families invited to an in-house ceremony at the end of a prestigious project so they can see for themselves the finished product? Does the company produce and distribute to its employees DVDs chronicling a major project so the employee's children can watch mom and dad being interviewed and better understand their important role in the project? Does the company publish project scrapbooks—with dramatic photographs of its employees at work—that can be displayed on the living room coffee table with pride? Are meaningful souvenirs provided upon completion of a big job? Are industry-related toys made for the children of the employees that (besides being fun to play with) help explain the core expertise of the company?

Though the numbers of new "recruits" who come from the families of employees may be small when compared to those joining the company from the general public, they can be significant as a moral force. Just as only a few rotten apples can spoil the barrel, a small number of employees who are sympathetic to the corporation can help maintain the integrity of the company culture. That culture, embodied by the parents, can be perpetuated by the children, who have grown up under the sheltering wings of the company.

It might be interesting to stand before a roomful of employees and ask for a show of hands to this question: "How many of you want your son or daughter to follow in your footsteps in this company?" Chances are very few hands would float into the air. To be fair, all parents want more for their children than the fruits of their own life experience. But FBI agents want the best for their kids too, and they are well aware of what the world has to offer the next generation in terms of salaries and perks. Yet ask this very same question of a roomful of agents and it is very likely the air would be picketed with hands. They would be pleased as punch to have a son or daughter in the Bureau, even though there are very many careers that offer more financial reward.

The question every CEO has to ask, then, is, "Does employment in my company add to the self-esteem of my employees?"

It is absolutely the case that working for certain organizations adds to the self-image of their employees. There is a world of difference between sharing the excitement of being associated with an industry leader, or with a dynamic start-up out to *become* an industry leader, and taking a paycheck from a loosely connected, passionless, leaderless outfit. Although it might be difficult for every company in private enterprise to cultivate the level of employee passion that flourishes in the FBI, every organization can do better than it is doing today in terms of increasing its attraction to the next generation of employees. The first step is to recognize that the kids who are currently perfecting their skateboard technique and their hairdos are already telling their friends whom they want to work for when they get out of school, and those aspirations are based on their perceptions of which organizations offer the challenge, excitement, and prestige they already crave.

Special Agent Marlo McGuire remembers the day the FBI came to her classroom. "An FBI recruiter came to our eighth-grade class and talked about all the things they do. My mom was an agent, and suddenly I realized, through him, all the exciting things she did. I raised my hand and asked if he knew my mom. He did! And he talked about her in front of the whole class. I was so proud. After that, I was the coolest kid in school for at least a week."

It is likely that many Fortune 500 companies would consider an outreach to eighth graders to be a bit of a stretch. Not the FBI. "We want to let these kids know about the FBI at an early age," explains agent Ethel McGuire, "because they have to be good citizens all through their youth in order to qualify. We wanted to give them something to target." Surely a company can give a child something to target as well.

Obviously, the Bureau is thinking long term. The average age of a newly hired agent is thirty; an eighth grader is thirteen and won't be a prospective employee for seventeen years! It would be a true testimonial to the vision of a "visionary" CEO if his or her company reached out to the next generation of employees, who wouldn't be eligible to join the company until long after the CEO's own tenure.

Hire Well

One of the best ways to prepare for tomorrow is to bring the best possible employees into the organization today. Time after time the FBI agents I interviewed expressed their unmitigated confidence in the future because, among other things, "we hire well." They are referring to the screening process that winnows out all but a tiny percentage of the tens of thousands of applicants annually, and also to the extensive background checks done on all likely candidates.

Neither of these processing techniques can be emulated by the business community. Most companies do not have the luxury of tens of thousands of eager applicants banging on the doors, nor the resources to screen out all but the best. And certainly "background checks" in private enterprise are limited to the barest essentials on the résumé—such as dates of previous employment, formal education, and relevant skills—which can scarcely be confirmed without anxiety, much less investigated. It is true that an applicant may sign a release that allows the hiring company to dig a little deeper, but that doesn't relieve the *previous* employer of anxiety. The previous employer knows full well that a rejected candidate can, through the Freedom of

Information Act, find out who gave him or her a "bad rap" and file a lawsuit in consequence. A number of questions are downright illegal to ask, while many others are so uncomfortable that they remain unexpressed for fear of litigation. We are afraid to ask the previous employer whether or not an applicant was a self-starter, a leader, etc. And were we to ask, the previous employer would feel constrained in answering.

But there is one FBI hiring practice that the business community *can* emulate: a candidate interview process that is truly a rite of passage.

"After the Phase One written test," explains Academy leadership instructor Jeff Green, "the applicant then has to go through an interview process conducted by a board of experienced street agents who take these interviews very, very seriously. These agents look you in the eye and ask probing questions that are designed to reveal an applicant's leadership qualities, work ethic, and character. It's pretty serious."

The interview experience is never forgotten by those who have been through it.

"I was getting out of the Marine Corps in 1979," recalls former undercover agent and twenty-six-year veteran Bob Hamer, "so I applied to both the CIA and the FBI. My first interview with a CIA representative was in a large room that had two folding chairs and absolutely no other furniture. The man conducting the interview had a scar stretching from ear to ear. Despite his forbidding appearance, his questions were very general in nature and it seemed more like a meet and greet.

"The FBI interview was a completely different experience. I sensed the importance of the interview immediately but had no idea what to expect, and I was nervous. Three FBI agents, all men, conducted the interview. Although friendly, they were all business. The small talk was minimal. I recall questions like 'Name a time you had to challenge authority,' and 'What was the most challenging assignment you ever had?' and 'You have a law degree and experience as a judge advocate in the Marine Corps. Why would you choose a career in the FBI?' and 'If the FBI doesn't offer you a position, what do you intend to do?' I did the best I could but I had no idea what they wanted.''

Former undercover agent and twenty-six-year FBI veteran Jack García remembers it this way: ''There were three agents, all guys. I was an imposing figure, having played college football, but they weren't intimidated—at all. They were polite, but their faces were cold. One agent asked me questions, while another seemed to be watching my body language as I answered, while the other seemed to be sizing me up. The questions seemed to focus on my resourcefulness. They wanted to know how enterprising I'd been in college and in my employment. They took notes. I got the impression they were writing down the things they liked about me. But it was only an impression, because they didn't smile.''

Later, Jack, during his career with the FBI, sat on the other side of the interviewing desk. He knows now exactly what those agents were looking for then. ''These were agents from the street. They were looking at me and asking themselves, 'Do I want to work with this person? Do I want to go through a door with this guy? Do I want him with me when I arrest a fugitive or get into a shoot-out? Is this guy going to watch my back?' ''

Female applicants are treated no differently. When Ethel McGuire walked into her interview, she was already an executive in a male-dominated business culture and knew how to handle herself. ''I think they were trying to find out if I was timid, because if you are, you can get killed out on the street. Three male agents interviewed me—polite, professional, Hoover-era-type individuals. At that time, twenty years ago, there weren't many female agents in the Bureau, and a lot of male agents didn't think 'girls' could handle the physical and mental stress of chasing bank robbers, kidnappers, and gangbangers. One of the men looked me up and down—all 115 pounds of me—and asked, 'How are you going to kick in a door?' "

Ethel smiles at the recollection. "I told him I wouldn't be able to *kick in* the door, but that I'd know what to do once the door was opened and I went through."

As in the case of the Medals Board, this is another example of FBI headquarters deferring to the judgment of streetwise field agents. The candidate is not interviewed by HR types from Washington, D.C., or by subcontracted support personnel such as psychologists or performance analysts. The person-to-person evaluation is left to those who actually know what to look for— the street agents themselves, who are, incidentally, experts at "interrogation." The candidate is actually facing the team he or she wishes to join, without intermediaries. They want to become FBI street agents, and they are interviewed by FBI street agents.

A great many companies, however, subcontract the recruiting and selection process out to third parties. "Headhunters," who may have never performed the duties that will be required of the applicant and who have never lived and breathed the particular corporate culture being represented, are the ones who are empowered to make the call. Some organizations will make use of their own HR personnel, who are, in a sense, professional interviewers, always mindful of all the questions they *cannot* ask the applicant. The HR recruiters at least have the virtue of being employees, but HR people generally have not "walked the walk." They are perfectly capable of describing the benefits offered by the company, but inexperienced as to the actual duties required of the candidate. Furthermore, there is a kind of con-spiratorial flavor to an interview with HR. The applicant wants to "get in" and the HR rep wants to get the applicant in.

But being interviewed by a board of top performers from the "front lines" of the marketplace would be a sobering experience indeed for the applicant, especially if the questions being asked had less to do with specific skills and much more to do with personal character. The nature of the probing questions would alert the candidate to the expectations of the company. For ex-ample, if an individual hoping to join the sales department were to be asked questions relating to the ethical dilemmas she has faced and dealt with—as opposed to how well she has exceeded her sales quotas in the past—she would get the definite message that honesty and integrity were of paramount importance to this particular organization. Moreover, she would see it, personified in the behavior of the "corporate soldiers" interviewing her. Their gravitas would either impress her favorably and instill a desire to be part of the team or send a signal that this might not be a good organizational match for her habitual sales pitch.

Just as a candidate for the FBI begins, during the interview, to get a sense of the awesome responsibilities of being an agent, so can the applicant to any organization begin to realize what he or she is getting into—*if* the interview is conducted by the cream of the crop of the company. It will, in fact, be a discovery process. At some point the candidate will realize, "So *this* is what they're looking for!" Such revelations are rare, if not im-possible, in the presence of headhunters or HR reps.

Let us imagine, for a moment, that the job candidate is clever enough to say what he thinks his interrogators want to hear and tells it so well and does such a thorough "snow job" that he is believed. Even then, the seriousness of the interview process will temper his moment of triumph. The consciousness of being an impostor who has joined a team of good men and women on false pretenses will haunt him and either eventually drive him away or goad him to better himself so that he eventually belongs on his own merits. This kind of interview "aftereffect" is impossible with headhunters or with HR people, because they too are part of the job-hunting game. But a board of top performers that has tried to look into your heart and has subsequently placed its trust in you and has welcomed you into the brotherhood places a special obligation to validate that trust. It is true that we are all on our best behavior during a job interview, but "best behavior" can become a habit, and an interview in the style of the FBI can inspire in the candidate a desire to be worthy.

Of course, another benefit to having top performers from the front lines evaluate the candidate is that they are in the best position to *answer* questions as well as ask them. The applicant will find himself or herself in the presence of those who actually do the job he or she is applying for. Why should this be a revolutionary concept? And yet how often are interviews conducted in this manner in private enterprise? Companies have become so frightened of lawsuits from rejected or "misled" applicants that they have divested themselves of the supreme duty of choosing who will face the challenges of the future on behalf of the organization. So anxious are they to be able to demonstrate, after the fact, that each applicant has been thoroughly informed of the benefits package, and has acknowledged the sexual harassment policy, and has understood the performance metrics, and realizes just how many vacation days are due him or her that it is almost as if the company is being interviewed by the candidate.

Make the Training Relevant to Future Challenges

When undercover agent Tom Zyckowski walked into the warehouse office, he sensed there was something wrong. The organized crime family he had infiltrated had accepted him as one of their own, but on this particular day there was a new face in the room, and the face was looking at him curiously. Tom made his greetings to the "businessmen," who were at that moment shuffling through bills of lading as they supervised the shipment of tons of stolen goods, when the new face suddenly lit up with recognition.

"Your name is Tom, isn't it?"

"Yeah, Tommy Zucco. How you doin'?"

"I think I know you. Aren't you from Belleville?"

"No way. Atlantic City."

"I knew a Tom from Belleville," pursued the stranger, "who looked a lot like you. He became a state trooper."

At this point, the eyes of the other men in the room glanced up with interest. The veteran FBI undercover agent turned his big frame on the newcomer and laughed in his face. "I don't know who you're talking about, pal," he said, "but he must have been pretty good-looking if he looks like me. I've been in a couple of state trooper cars, but always in the backseat," he joked, "never the front."

Snorting with laughter, the men in the room returned to their paperwork. The crisis had passed.

Tom Zyckowski can laugh at that "near death" experience in retrospect. "That was a tight spot," he readily admits. "I was unarmed in a room with at least four guys carrying guns, and one of them recognized me. What separates a good undercover agent from a bad one," he grins, "is that he doesn't turn to jelly when the heat is on."

Tom credits much of his ability to deal with the unexpected to the realistic training he received in FBI undercover school: "They constantly place you in scenarios where you have to think on your feet. For example, a 'bad guy' will insist you snort some cocaine with him, or in another scenario puts a gun to your head and accuses you of being a cop. The simulations were utterly realistic. The trainers and the trainees so thoroughly believed in the scenarios that occasionally fistfights broke out between them. That's how realistic it was! A lot of guys—halfway through the course—would decide that being an undercover agent was not for them. The stress was just too great."

The mark of a "relevant" training program is when a twenty-five-year veteran undercover agent, who has experienced more than his share of close calls, credits *schooling* with his survival on the mean streets of Newark, New Jersey!

Ethel McGuire, who worked gangs and drugs for thirteen years before becoming the assistant special agent in charge (ASAC) of the Los Angeles field office's counterterrorism squad, can attest with some humor to the relevance of the Academy training.

"One of the agents I've mentored is a female who expressed some shock that her instructors at Quantico, in certain training scenarios, were using four-letter words. She told me that she expected the FBI to be more 'professional' than that. I told her, 'Honey, the people you're going to be dealing with out on the streets aren't going to be using the *Oxford English Dictionary*. The role players are preparing you for what you're going to hear in the real world. Get over it.' And she did," laughs Ethel.

Firearms training as well is conducted with vivid real-life scenarios in mind. "In the old days," explains Rob Grant, "shooting at the range was what we called 'position shooting,' and all that counted was hitting the bull's-eye from a fixed stance. Since then we've transitioned to more situational training, where you're firing on the move through a combat course or from the inside of a vehicle, because these are the real 'positions' our agents will be in on the street."

There is a widely shared perception in American society that institutions of learning in general do not sufficiently prepare today's youth for the challenges they are sure to confront later in life, "when reality hits." And it is no different in the business world. Training is considered necessary, of course, in order to learn the basics, but many employees continue to believe that the basic skills are learned on the job and not in a classroom. They believe, further, that the corporate training department is as much of an ivory tower as the academic university.

No one has ever accused the FBI Academy of being an ivory tower.

Obviously, in the business environment, the employee's perception of the relevancy of the corporate training program is nearly as important as the curriculum offered. If the rank-and-file members don't believe in the applicability of the skills being taught, they won't attend the voluntary classes or pay attention during the required courses. Management's first concern, therefore, should be to determine if its employees are right.

Too often the training department is at the bottom of the totem pole when it comes to resource allocation and company prestige. Rather than take their top performers off the front lines, and away from the customer so they can teach what they know, many companies ask retiring or already retired employees to pass on their knowledge, as if teaching were simply a matter of telling war stories around the campfire. Although there is certainly value in learning the perspective of old-timers, a dynamic training program requires certified instructors at the peak of their powers who habitually look ahead, not in retrospect. FBI Academy instructors are precisely that—experienced agents right off the street, whose mission is to prepare the newcomers for the dangers they have recently faced.

One of those instructors is Jeff Green. Before joining the Bureau, he was a city police officer. He remembers his first day on the job, fresh from police academy: "I hopped into the passenger side of the squad car, and the sergeant at the steering wheel turned to me with a face of stone and said, 'I'm not your friend. I'm here to train you and to evaluate you. And I can tell you right now: forget all that crap you learned at the police academy.'"

Even worse than the sergeant's advice was Jeff's reaction. "Unfortunately," he says, with a wry smile, "I was kind of excited. I felt as if I had been welcomed into the real world of police work and that I was about to be initiated into the clique of streetwise veterans. I didn't realize what a blunder the sergeant had made by pulling the rug out from under all the training I had received at the academy. And by the way, he was wrong. Most of what I learned was totally relevant to the street."

The larger question is, "Why did the sergeant have such contempt for the training program of his own organization?" Had he personally found it irrelevant? If so, why hadn't Jeff Green also found it irrelevant in his ensuing years with that police department? Certainly it is fashionable for "hard-boiled" veterans to express disdain for just about anything that represents headquarters. It is likely the sergeant groused over many other manifestations of the bureaucracy, such as official policy bulletins issued from on high, certain "undeserved" promotions into the ranks of leadership, supervisors who cared more about paperwork than about their own people, the police psychologists, the health care benefits, retirement plan, etc., etc. The police academy may have just been another embodiment of an organizational structure that did not seem welcoming to him.

Having had his police training disparaged by fellow police officers, Jeff is determined not to let that happen to his budding FBI leaders. "The way we train here at the FBI Academy," he reveals, "is in accordance with the reality in the field. When these young men and women get out onto the street, it's not like they have to shuck their 'academic' training and learn the 'street-smart way.' They already know the street-smart way, because they've learned it here."

Companies would do well to emulate FBI training by selecting and certifying their trainers from the front lines of the marketplace. Top performers, at their peak earning capacity, can be tapped on the shoulder for a tour of duty as an instructor—with compensatory pay and a boost in prestige for making the sacrifice. The new trainee, like the FBI Academy student, will see the "real thing" at the front of the class, which means an implicit mentoring program will have begun *before* the student has assumed his or her job responsibilities.

Rather than simply teach out of a training manual, the instructor should invite key customers to share with the new employees how their company saved the day with an innovative, creative solution that the competition had been unable to provide. Students can also be encouraged to keep pace with the rapid developments within the industry by bringing in and discussing pertinent articles, books, and blog postings each day. Realistic simulations requiring the total involvement and commitment of the student should replace the lecture format, which allows students to "drift away" while seeming to listen. And the course curriculum—so often unchanged from year to year on the assumption that "the basics" are immutable—

should be updated annually, so that the applications of these "immutable" fundamentals are consistently tested for relevancy.

When corporate boot camp is acknowledged by the company's top performers years later as the source of their continued success in the field, the company will have achieved the goal of a relevant training program. The challenge then is to keep it relevant.

Cultivate Flexibility of Mind

During his twenty-six years as an undercover agent, Bob Hamer often had to live by his wits and follow his instincts. "As an undercover agent, you walk the high wire alone," he reveals. "You're the one who has to make instantaneous decisions. You can't wait for a committee decision."

One of his biggest cases, code-named Smoking Dragon, began as a counterfeit cigarette investigation. But, like an explorer poking his head through the entrance of a cave, Hamer sensed unanticipated dimensions. The "cigarette" case expanded into an investigation of a drug-smuggling operation, which then expanded into an international weapons cartel investigation, which then led to the recovery of millions of dollars of counterfeit bills manufactured by a foreign government. For nearly three years, the enterprising agent infiltrated a menacing global organization from the ground up. He began by dealing with street thugs and finished the case "doing business" with high-level military and organized crime figures from three countries.

During a critical point in the undercover investigation,

one of the ladies in the criminal enterprise happened to take a fancy to him. "I'd attend business meetings in my role," he explains, "gathering all the information I could, and one of the female subjects started being friendly and sitting next to me. I couldn't afford any affectionate attention from her because I was wired for sound."

So at the next scheduled meeting, Bob Hamer brought a female agent with him posing as his girlfriend. Not only did that discourage the affections of the lady in question, it proved to be the springboard for yet another innovation.

Hamer soon had an opportunity to close the deal for a major weapons shipment, but the money he needed for the down payment exceeded his budget. Since there didn't seem to be a conventional solution, he invented a story, virtually on the spur of the moment. "I told them," he grins, "that my wife found out about the 'girlfriend' and hit the roof. I told them she had filed for divorce and that I was unable, because of a restraining order, to get the funds they wanted for the deal. So I offered them instead an escrow letter committing money from a stock fund, which they finally accepted. So I made an international weapons deal without using any actual money."

No doubt agent Hamer's acting ability served him well as he made his unusual offer, but so did the mental flexibility cultivated during his years with the Bureau. It is a fact that the FBI, which requires of its agents a plan for just about everything, spends much of its training time promoting the ability to think outside the plan.

The FBI does not want its agents so committed to a single strategy that they would be flabbergasted by an unanticipated turn of events. The dynamics of an investigation, or of a dangerous takedown, have been known to turn on a dime, and agents must be able to think on their feet. To further complicate matters, there is always the possibility that agents will have to formulate an action plan based on information they themselves find questionable but nonetheless worthy of pursuing. They may choose to venture out onto thin ice, treading lightly, with their eyes wide open.

This is why in basic training at the Academy and periodically throughout their careers, agents go through simulation training that is essentially a series of surprises. On the tactical ranges, figures representing lethal threats pop up, as do others representing innocent bystanders. The agent must think fast. His or her score depends on it, and a poor score is not taken lightly by the instructors. If the agent mistakenly "shoots" an innocent bystander, that paper target represents an embarrassing failure of judgment and perhaps a fatally flawed ability to discriminate threats quickly. Similarly, agents in training might be purposely given wrong information prior to a simulated mission just to see how they will react to a sudden and dramatic change in expectations.

Throughout their careers, FBI agents are put through "what-if?" scenarios. Frequent drills are held, no matter how busy the workload, not only to develop crisis-management skills but to induce a kind of stoic acceptance of whatever the universe has to offer. After a while the "surprises" cease to surprise, because the mind has been conditioned not to count on certain reactions by the suspect or on the consequential unfolding of events, but to remain open to all possibilities.

It would seem that in the business community—if one goes by the articles, interviews, and expert commentary in the news—that "having a plan" is considered by many to be nearly the equivalent of reaching one's goals. There is a reverence for grand strategy that borders on plan worship.

That may be because the very process of crafting a thoughtful strategy inspires confidence. The labor put into investigating the workings of the marketplace, the sight of wise heads concurring over the implications of accumulated data, the resources put into place to enable the plan, can make a task force, if it is not sufficiently humble, believe that the grand strategy has by the magic of intention been incorporated into reality. It's just human nature. Craving order, we tend to embrace a carefully considered strategy that seems to impose a measure of control over events that cannot be controlled. The more thoroughly we plan, the more invested we become in the plan. And once we fall in love with the plan, everything we see in the marketplace will be interpreted as a confirmation of our conviction, just as a boy who has been slapped by an indignant girl thinks, "She loves me!" Market threats will not be recognized because they do not fit the future we have created for ourselves. Warnings and contrary advice from associates will be considered heresy because the plan—not the marketplace—has become reality. That we've also come up with "contingency" plans should not cause us to overlook the fact that the master plan is itself contingent upon events we only expect to take place.

Having flexibility of mind in business situations can mean the difference between success and failure. And very often the newcomer to the organization is more mentally agile simply because he or she has not yet fallen under the spell of the company's perspective on the world. The corporate plan, and the propaganda that accompanies it, can have a leveling effect on the imagination and IQ of the workforce. After a while, we all have a tendency to look at business opportunities in terms of how they cross over into our capabilities instead of how we can adapt to rush out and meet them. A salesperson who has studied his product, has become an expert on his product, and has fallen in love with his product will see the world through the prism of that product's features and benefits, and thus literally not see opportunities just outside the reach of that perspective. So rather than listening to the needs of his customer, he talks—or impatiently waits to talk—about the virtues of his product. If certain expectations of the customer are not met, he will try to diminish those expectations instead of acknowledging their legitimacy and striving to fulfill them.

A company can emulate the FBI's program to cultivate mental flexibility and to discourage plan worship with its own version of "pop-up targets" and surprise scenarios: frequent "brainstorming" sessions that are fun and stimulating.

A manager could host a brainstorming lunch (which in itself will attract attendees). Actual thinking caps could be provided to liven up the party. The focus of the session could be a question, such as "If you worked for a competitor, how would you sell against us?" or "If you were the CEO, what changes would you make?" The group could be asked to offer suggestions for a company Super Bowl commercial.

Plans gone awry could be experienced in what-if? scenarios, such as "Your multimedia presentation crashes, and there is no tomorrow. What do you do?" or "The customer seems ready to buy the product, but his IT guru, who has his own agenda, keeps raising off-the-wall objections. What do you do?" Philosophical themes could be explored with questions like "Why is sales an honorable profession?" The lunch could be devoted to a SWOT (strengths, weaknesses, opportunities, threats) analysis. Or the session could be a fanciful team effort in which the individuals, superheroes all, assign each other appropriate superpowers.

Of course, the brainstorming session certainly could be case specific, enlisting the help of all in attendance on a "real-life" company conundrum. The important thing in that kind of session would be to invite all comers, not just those in the department confronting the challenge, so the perspectives will be fresh and possibly delightfully unanticipated. The rules must be "anything goes." No suggestion will be considered "dumb" and all will be written down by the facilitator at the whiteboard.

Employees who participate in brainstorming sessions will feel invigorated afterward, and not just intellectually. These can be emotionally satisfying experiences because of the good humor and the sense of camaraderie engendered. Brainstorming sessions can also inspire confidence in one's associates, as individuals distinguish themselves with verve and imagination. One begins to feel that with so many minds considering the issue, surely it will be resolved. Sometimes the "surprises" will not be in the solutions but in the revelations of personality. The timid may prove themselves to be "tigers" in abstract thought, and the taciturn may be discovered to have a dry, profound sense of humor. And the manager, who facilitates, can show himself or herself to be a good sport.

One of the great benefits of creative brainstorming sessions is that we all begin to question our own premises, our own habitual starting points as we approach a problem. Moreover, if the session is a free and happy one, we may question the company's premises as well. Sacred cows can be—if not eaten—at least milked. Questions like "Why do we allow our limited conception of our 'core expertise' to eternally define us in the marketplace?" can be seriously discussed without being considered blasphemy.

This also might be a good time for having stimulating and fun (remember attendance at these sessions is voluntary) exercises, almost like party games, that pit team against team in the search for consensus. "Groupthink" has been made out to be a bad thing in business books, as if "consensus" only drowns out meaningful dissent. But groupthink can be a marvelous experience, because it demands contribution, which draws the shy and timid out into the center of attention, where they gratefully bask. The synergy created by minds coming together for a good purpose can be breathtaking. It should happen again and again.

Participating employees will return to their desks with a smile and with a sense of the power of their own ability to seek and find solutions. The nice thing about these sessions is that critical thinking tends to be self-perpetuating. Suddenly one's work will seem less of a grind and more of a living experiment—something that might be improved upon. Salespeople, as they call on their customers, will be more agile of mind, quicker to suggest new ways to look at a problem and quicker to sense new opportunities. That's why regular brainstorming sessions must never come to be regarded as simulations that take place only within the four walls of the room, under the facilitation of the manager, but rather as springboards for practical application. This is why the manager-facilitator must be alert to really good suggestions and have them implemented. If the brainstorming sessions are looked upon by the participants as wishful-thinking episodes without occasional concrete application, the participants will lose interest (though they may continue to come for the free lunch).

The Problem with Success

As of this writing, the United States has not been attacked by terrorists since September 11, 2001. Or perhaps "successfully attacked" is a better way to phrase it, since terrorists have indeed plotted, prepared, and deployed—and thankfully have been interrupted through the combined efforts of the FBI and its affiliated agencies on the Joint Terrorism Task Force. The FBI has been so successful, in fact, that life seems to have returned to a pre-9/11 normalcy. The threat of international terrorism is less frequently a front-page newspaper story or a lead report on the nightly news, having been replaced by stories of misbehaving celebrities and the most recent winner on *American Idol.*

As the often unpublicized successes of the agency mount, there is a corresponding drop in the vigilance of the man in the street. No longer feeling quite as threatened as on the day when three thousand innocent American men, women, and children were murdered, citizens have noticeably relaxed. Because the FBI is vigilant, we are less so. We assume the FBI has the terror situation under control, and we go about our business much as we did before 9/11. Indeed, exit-polling data during the 2008 presidential primaries confirmed that the number one issue on the mind of the voter is the economy—not terror. And, of course, the great irony of the matter is that the FBI needs the eyes and ears of the citizen in the street more than ever. The FBI has been, in a very real sense, penalized for its success.

Companies, too, can be penalized for their success. Buoyed by impressive quarterly reports, exhilarated by the rising price of company stock, employees may feel swept along by a momentum that seems nearly self-perpetuating. The larger the organization, the more likely the employee is to underestimate his own contribution and to attribute the company's success to a visionary CEO, the hotshot salespeople who are in tight with all the major customers, and the R&D geniuses who continue to surprise the marketplace with unprecedented innovations. The CEO confirms this picture with his or her smile of confidence, and the future seems assured. In the minds of the employees, the successful company is a rocket ship, the CEO is its pilot, and they are the crew that performs the light maintenance required during the voyage.

Success doesn't necessarily breed complacency, but it can create an unwarranted sense of confidence in the leadership of the company, which can be almost as bad. Just as the FBI requires the vigilance of every citizen if it is to protect the nation from terrorist attack, the company's continued well-being depends on the employee's frank assessment of the threat-rich business environment in which he or she strives. The employee should never be allowed to underestimate the vulnerability of the company in the struggle for existence that characterizes the free market.

Nothing brings an organization together more quickly than a common threat. And the threats exist in plenty! Competitors want to drive us out of the market, customers are always looking for a better deal, the shareholders will jump ship at the slightest stumble, and the costs of doing business are disproportionately rising in relation to profits. But visionary CEOs do not want to share their troubles or appear unduly alarmed or distracted by the struggle for existence. Instead, they attempt to raise our gaze to a time in the future when the company will be the industry leader. Meanwhile the barbarians are at the gate.

Common cause is most easily recruited in response to common threat. Why do so many CEOs seem to think it would diminish their stature if they were to sound the alarm and ask the workforce to fight for the survival of the company? Because whether the company is a David or a Goliath, it's always a matter of survival. Most employees will acknowledge that *they* are only a couple of paychecks away from losing the house. Why shouldn't the CEO reveal the same truth about the company?

Because the same is true for all companies in a free market, the only difference being the number of "paychecks" required from the customer to keep the doors open. Why give the impression that the company is a self-perpetuating entity that simply has to be conscientiously maintained but not defended?

A little bit of fear can be a good thing. Fear of the future, for example, motivates us to save for a rainy day. A prudent fear of the unknown prompts us to sail carefully through uncharted waters. Fear, in fact, has served humankind rather well in its long history of evading saber-toothed tigers, making homes out of caves, protecting its young, and growing crops instead of chancing the nomadic life. And fear in the business environment serves a similar purpose; it keeps us on our toes. When success is taken for granted, the workforce loses touch with the struggle for existence and fails to recognize impending threats—or, worse yet, considers itself invulnerable to recognized threats.

There has to be a way employees at every level of the hierarchy can be gently reminded, now and again, of the company's vulnerability despite—and perhaps because of— its current success. Many successful companies in virtually every industry have been blindsided by the innovations of their competitors, and by market and legislative forces out of their control, at the very pinnacle of their success. These "war stories" should be told around the corporate campfires in detail so that every employee is stricken with the realization it can happen to his or her company as well.

A manager might even hold an exercise in which every person in the department is asked to update, and to turn in, his or her résumé, the manager included. Even though everyone would be assured that this was simply an exercise to make the dramatic point of the possible consequences of failure in the marketplace, the subconscious mind would accept the drill as something real.

Updating a résumé can be a sobering experience. The manager can relieve the tension by collecting all the résumés, placing them in a pile in the center of the room, and suggesting with a big smile, "Isn't it great we don't have to fax these out today?" A group discussion could follow in which each person would explore his or her role in the company's success as well as his or her interpretations of the threats emanating from the marketplace.

A similar dramatic point could be made by asking everyone to check the job boards over the weekend and to bring in a suitable match for his or her talents. Here again, it's just an exercise, but uncomfortable nonetheless. And true to life! Polishing up the résumé and going through the ordeal of job hunting are the unenviable consequences of a company failure. It goes without saying that these exercises should be reserved for times when the company is doing so well that its success is being taken for granted. It would be unnecessary and counterproductive to ask employees to go through these activities when the company was truly struggling. Presumably the point will have already been taken.

It is ironic that an impending company failure brings us face-to-face with personal responsibility, while good times lull us into, if not dependency on the "top performers," at the very least an underappreciation of our own contributions to success and of the importance of our continued efforts. We feel the thrill of success and it seems to us that the organization, having gained sufficient momentum, is unstoppable. All the forces of the marketplace seem aligned with its progress, like a happy horoscope. We feel virtually fated to succeed. And that is a moment of danger for the company. When we are confident that we are in good hands, we fold our own.

Conclusion

The powerful management principles revealed in this book cannot, though universally applicable, be taken completely out of context and cannot be entirely divorced from their source. The guiding decency of the men and women in the Bureau empower these principles, just as, to take an absurd case, the dishonesty of the Mafia would render these selfsame principles, if "practiced," powerless. A corrupt and cynical organization could not implement shared-goal exercises, for example, because customer satisfaction is not its primary objective, nor could it appeal to self-sacrifice if it didn't offer something beyond financial reward to its employees. To implement FBI management principles properly, the organization must try its best to be worthy of them.

A "one for all, all for one" corporate ethos is fine and dandy to talk about, but it is unattainable if the employees do not believe in the corporate mission. A paycheck does not constitute a common bond because paychecks can be gotten elsewhere. Similarly, a company that does not recognize the yearning of its employees for moral support when they have been mischaracterized on the evening news will turn the other cheek instead of fighting back against the media.

FBI management principles will work for similarly earnest organizations. They cannot be cynically applied, any more than bits and pieces of democracy can be selectively allocated within a totalitarian state—or any more than a U.S. Army leadership manual, picked up on the battlefield, could be used by a terrorist commander to inspire his fighters. It's not the mere implementation that makes FBI management principles so effective. It is the spirit of the organization that illuminates and fulfills them.

If it happens that your company is not quite up to par with the model used throughout this book, it may be that these management principles will prove to be transformative at first, and subsequently effective on the competitive battlefield of the marketplace.

Afterword

In this book, I focused on the management principles practiced by the FBI that I thought would be powerful tools for the business community. But the reader may be a little curious to know, at this point, if there was any area where I felt the FBI could learn from the business community.

And, yes, there is—in the realm of human resources.

The FBI's mandatory retirement age of fifty-seven seems too young, because not all agents wait that long. Seeing the handwriting on the wall and being eligible for full retirement benefits before the age of fifty-seven, many agents who have never bought a home during their nomadic careers, and who now have kids in college, are forced to make an economic choice.

"One of the biggest problems with the FBI," believes retired agent and former FBI inspector Tim McNally, "is that they lose their best people in their early fifties. The FBI spends more time training its people—with management programs, leadership schools, special technical training, etc. But since they're eligible to leave after twenty years, private industry will scoop up good people from the FBI in a heartbeat. So just when somebody peaks in terms of their management and leadership capabilities, some other organization gets the benefit of that investment in time."

Good for private industry, but bad for the FBI.

Tom Zyckowski, with twenty-five years of invaluable experience, retired from the Bureau at a robust fifty-four years of age.

"It's more of a marketability issue," he explains, "that agents don't wait until they're fifty-seven before they go into private enterprise."

In its defense, the FBI isn't like other organizations when it comes to the responsibilities of the profession. The Bureau does not want sixty-year-old agents charging up flights of stairs in pursuit of a fugitive, or getting into a back-alley gunfight in the middle of the night wearing trifocals. It is a testimonial to the FBI's ethos, "Every agent is an investigator," that the Bureau takes this view.

But surely it is possible to retain leadership positions in the organization for those agents who, though fifty-seven years old ("youthful" by Japanese standards!), are deemed by management to still be in their prime. Maybe these experienced, wise, invaluable managers could turn in their guns but not their badges. Surely there is room for them at the strategic roundtable in this time of peril.

Fifty-five-year-old Assistant Director Stephen Tidwell is very close to that mandatory retirement age. He is fit as a fiddle and an accomplished executive. Private industry is not unaware of his capabilities—and of his impending availability.

"I've had job offers, but I'm staying," he reveals.

"We're still at war."

Index